SPEAKING IN THE SHOWER

Presentation Skills Exposed

PAULA SMITH

Copyright © Paula Smith 2010
Published by Allsouth Pty Ltd
Edited by Jonquil Brooks, Brick Cat Editing - www.brickcat.net
Illustrations by Malcolm Lindsay, Scribbles Illustration Studio
First published 2010
First edition

ISBN 978-0-9807256-0-5

Printed by Success Print, 7A Goongarrie St, Bayswater, W.A. 6053

Acknowledgements

Thank you...

To my loving and supportive family for giving me time away from you to complete my book. My husband Darren who loves me unconditionally and supports me in everything I do; my best friend, daughter and light of my life Sarah; my son Danny whose heart and soul are a gift to be treasured forever; and my beautiful, energetic daughter Princess Chloe, our little miracle.

To every one of my students over the past two decades who have shared their speaking experiences with me and have unknowingly contributed to Speaking in the Shower.

To David Koutsoutkis, Kevin Tibble and Peter Dhu who have shared their speaking journey within the pages of this book.

To Malcolm, Jonquil and Jeff who helped me get my book to print. Your suggestions, illustrations and personal commitment made it all so much fun.

Contents

COMMON SPEAKING TERMS: BEFORE

D efinitions of common speaking terms *before* you take the Speaking in the Shower journey

Presentation – Something that some people do to get attention

Audience – A group of hungry animals ready to pounce at any moment

Fear – An overwhelming feeling I get as I walk in front of a group of hungry animals

Sleep – A rare occurrence any time up to a week or even a month prior to any presentation

Hyperventilation – A natural bodily function that occurs when somebody asks you to speak

Lectern – Lectern?? No, not sure I have heard that term

Visual Aid – I know that one… My glasses

Presentation Opportunity – An opportunity to delegate to others

Survival – Something that may or may not occur prior to, during or after a speech

Key Message – Where the toilets and fire escape are

Applause – Something I do for everyone else

Name Recall – Mine, a skill I sometimes forget in very stressful situations

PowerPoint – Is that like needle point?

Credibility Statement – Mr Jones asked me to talk to you all today, as I was the only one not going to the staff party

Humour – Jokes, jokes and more jokes

Presenter Style – How the presenter looks

Presentation Structure – Is that the lectern word?

If there is no passion in your life, then have you really lived? Find your passion, whatever it may be. Become it and let it become you and you will find great things happen for you, to you, because of you

T. Alan Armstrong

FOREWORD

Think about all the presentations that you have been to and the presenters who have stood up, spoken out and delivered them. Perhaps it was a sales pitch presentation, a high school principal's address, a conference, a training session, or maybe you were at your sister's wedding watching the comedian entertainer or the sensational MC. Which ones stood out?

I am sure you can think of some dreadful speakers straightaway – the ones where you are begging for them to finish, or worse, secretly hoping that the speaker comes in contact with the chandelier hanging from the roof. What was it about that speaker that made you switch off and want to run from the room? What about the exceptional presenter? The one that left you feeling inspired; the speech that made you want to go out and change something in your life immediately; the speech that touched your emotions; the speaker who was speaking for hours and you just didn't want them to stop. Not all speakers are good looking, energetic, charismatic individuals, so what is it about these speakers that provided you with an experience that moved you, inspired you or persuaded you at long last to take action?

In the pages of Speaking in the Shower I aim to give you some knowledge and share some tips, stories and skills to help you become a memorable speaker. They are strategies that everyone can learn to become a speaking superstar – a speaker who stands up and speaks out in their own style, in their own way, to share their message; a speaker who is comfortable, confident, passionate and authentic.

A Bit About Me...

I have never had a deep fear of public speaking. Don't get me wrong... Did I feel anxiety? Did I get nervous? Did I get the sweaty palms? Sure, but I was still one of those kids begging for opportunities to run the school assembly or be the race caller at the annual sports carnival. In fact, any opportunity to perform or speak in front of an audience was eagerly accepted.

One could say I was just oozing with confidence or perhaps liked the sound of my own voice, but I was just a normal kid with the normal hang-ups of many a teenager, confident with my peers and still a little reserved with strangers and others considered to be "important people". Unless I was on the stage. Then it was my floor and I loved the nerves, the anticipation and the adrenalin before a performance, the exhilaration of being on stage, and got high on the accolades I received when the performance was over.

It didn't occur to me that my peers, my teachers and perhaps my mum's bank manager didn't feel the same way. I found it fascinating. How could someone fear talking? Why didn't these people look for opportunities to say their piece? Why is the fear of speaking such a high ranking category in the list of what people fear the most? This question has led me on a 20-year journey to find out why people fear public speaking and what they can do to overcome the fear and actually enjoy the experience. A journey that has seen me work with thousands of children, teenagers and adults to help them with their communication and speaking skills

My mum introduced me to amateur theatre when I was nine years of age (in my first performance I was Leticia Lettuce at the Vegetable Wedding – you can only imagine my costume) and then with my mum and sister I spent the next 10 years performing in musicals and stage dramas, as a family affair. Dad came to watch but the thought of standing on a stage was enough to make his stomach churn (as some of you can relate to).

As a teenager at school – yes, you can imagine – I chose all the drama subjects and anything to do with speaking and presenting. I loved a good debate too. So when I was elected the President of the Student Council I was ecstatic. I got to MC every school assembly, prepare speeches and speak on behalf of the school – I was in my element.

When I left school at 15, like many 15-year-olds I didn't have a clue what I wanted to do. I tried so many things, from shoe sales, office work, an accountant's office (that was a hoot), journalism, computers (definitely not my area as I discovered), then I tried some modelling classes and I was hooked. All those bright lights, new clothes and an audience; it was great. But I could never make up my mind whether I wanted to model or be the compère, and having to socialise in the land of the beautiful people was also a bit of a drain.

From job to job I went, trying everything and anything I could, never quite fitting in, nothing really fed my passions, nothing got me excited about jumping out of bed in the morning and springing off to work. I think I was destined for small business from an early age. I was a 17-year-old who finally decided what I wanted to be. I wanted to be the boss. Now that got me excited. (With no experience and no qualifications – in my 17-year-old wisdom I thought why not, how hard can it be?)

So I enrolled in a small-business course and within 12 months of finishing my course I had started a business in the only thing I knew – talking and modelling. So there it was: "A kids' personal development and modelling school".

A business that ended up being the largest of its kind in the country.

For the next 20 years I had the opportunity to teach thousands of children and adults public speaking and performing skills. Although I called the business a Modelling Academy all of the programmes were based on real life skills and personal development.

If you told a 13-year-old they were going to classes to learn basic communication and life skills there would have been few or no enrolments. By adding the catwalk, performing and fashion into the courses, it proved the perfect recipe for happy kids and happy parents.

The programme model was soon franchised, giving more children access to the personal development programmes I had created. As I mentioned, we were not a traditional modelling school, our teachers were trained at our head office which also became a registered training organisation, and if you popped into one of our classrooms it was not an unusual sight to see a wheelchair or some crutches or other unusual instruments as many of our kids had special needs. Everyone was welcome and thousands and thousands of students gained the skills to hold their heads high with confidence and speak publicly at student graduations in front of huge audiences.

Many a parent told us that little Johnny would never stand up and speak, but little Johnny always did. We just kept the nervous mums and dads away from them on performance nights.

I was very passionate about teaching these skills not only to kids but anyone who wanted to learn them. So our ages ranged from 3 to 70. Many mums and grandparents thought it was so unfair that the kids were getting all the fun. Then the parents of the kids introduced our programmes into their organisations and into the schools and it grew and grew. I learnt a great deal by teaching such a wide range of ages and from all walks of life. So much in fact... well I could write a book on it... You can learn a lot from a three-year-old with no fear or a junior teen very concerned all of a sudden about what everybody else thinks.

I also needed to continually develop my own skills so I could pass new methodologies and new skills to my instructors and to the students.

So the journey began. I enrolled and completed a degree in training and development, and started to write nationally accredited programmes on personal development. Over these years, I studied, I evaluated and I talked to my students about their joys and fears of public speaking and performing.

Based on the experiences over this time, and now with my new training business (training trainers and presenters), I wanted to put on paper what I have learnt over this time. A handbook, a guide, a light and entertaining insight into how to present in public if you really are truly terrified or if you just want to develop your presentation skills to really get your message across effectively and professionally.

Speaking in the Shower is for anyone who has been invited to stand up and speak out – the teacher, the trainer, the salesperson, the charity worker, the friend who has been nominated to be the MC at the family wedding, in fact anyone who wants to get a message across to an audience, whether it be an audience of two or 2000. If you are planning to be a professional speaker or presenter you may wish to consider this book as your apprenticeship.

The Speaking in the Shower term came from listening to my husband and kids singing in the shower at the top of their lungs, as if they were all rock stars. A daily concert in the Smith household. Could you get my husband to speak in front of two people? Never. As he would say, he would rather chop wood in a hail storm all day than speak for two minutes. So why is it that in the shower you lose your inhibitions, considering you are also naked…? How can you get that shining star to step out from the shower and onto a platform in front of a real live audience, still oozing the same charm, charisma and confidence?

Please turn the pages and let me share the journey with you from speaking in the shower to speaking on the platform to real people (with your clothes on).

Our character is what we do when we think no one is looking

H. Jackson Brown, Jr.

1. SPEAKING IN THE SHOWER – WHY IT'S SO EASY WITH MY RUBBER DUCKIE

When you are singing in the shower at the top of your lungs do you really care how good it is? Are you singing to be judged on your performance techniques or voice control? Of course not, you are just doing your thing, having a bit of fun and not really thinking of the outside world. Who cares if the words in the song are not the words you are singing? Who is going to chastise you for the la, la, la, la instead of the boogie woogie do da?

In the shower there are no demands, no judgments, no fear, just you being you. What if it was that easy out there... out of the bathroom and in the real world?

But we are not singing now, we are speaking – that thing we do all day every day with our lips and tongue. We speak and communicate every day so why is it when you suddenly have an audience things change? The shaking starts, the palms start to sweat and all of a sudden what seemed liked the English language five minutes ago is starting to resemble some bizarre language from a far, far away land that has not yet been discovered.

Your audience is a group of people who can make you feel nervous, intimidated, even stupid, if you give them permission. They can also make you feel smart, charismatic, exciting, inspiring and downright sensational, if you give them permission.

It is not the audience we need to work with, it is you. It is your mind that fills up with crazy thoughts of a slow and painful death if one word is forgotten or if you can't answer a question that someone has posed.

The sensational superstar from the shower now has to move out of the shower and be the same charismatic individual. A confident individual with a message to share.

Presentation skills are now going to be exposed. Guess what? No secrets, no mystery just a powerful skill to learn, develop and enjoy.

You can speak well if your tongue can deliver a message of
your heart

John Ford

2. WHY ME?

Why Are You Speaking?

Have you been asked to say a speech at a function?? Have you been asked to chair the next meeting or perhaps deliver a sales presentation? Whatever the reason, you are speaking because someone out there – and it may even be you – has decided that you have something to say.

This guide is for anyone who wants to develop their presentation style, for anyone who wants to develop their communication skills to get their message across. School teachers, trainers, professional speakers, sales people, customer service representatives, keynote speakers at conferences, managers who need to address staff, school students who need to present their homework to the class… almost everyone at some stage in their life will find themselves in a position where they are in the spotlight.

If you need to communicate with others and present information, learning to speak in public is an essential tool for success.

It is not always the confident person who can speak in public; it is the skill of public speaking that makes the person confident when speaking.

As I discussed with you in the book's opening, I spent over 20 years teaching children to speak in front of an audience. It was a life skill that I thought was essential to include in any of our personal development programmes, whether you were three or 33. We teach our kids to be polite and always use their manners, we teach our kids to use time management strategies and we teach them personal hygiene. All very important. But do we, at the dinner table each night, teach them to talk to us? Do we teach them how to talk to others? Do we teach them the best way to get their message across?

Speaking in public should be one of those life skills we teach our kids. A vital communication skill.

And you can tell them to practise in the shower.

Speaking Is An Opportunity

Speaking is an opportunity – an opportunity to build a relationship, the most important thing in business today. Successful business is all about building long-term relationships. But how do you get an opportunity to start a new relationship? It is usually in the form of a meeting, a presentation, an opportunity to talk to someone who can make a decision.

Speaking is an opportunity to share with people who you are, what you do, what you have to offer and how you can help them. It is an opportunity to be noticed, to have some visibility in your social or professional circle.

It is an opportunity to share your knowledge, to teach a skill, to change behaviours.

If your mindset is "I like opportunities. How lucky am I to be in a position to share my message", we are already halfway there.

Purpose

When someone asks you to present it can be for a number of reasons. It could be to:

Entertain

Some people are natural entertainers. Because of your sharp wit and humour you may have been asked to be the guest speaker at a business function or the after-dinner speaker. Or perhaps you have been asked to address a group of high school students in a light and entertaining manner about your industry.

Once you know that *entertaining* is your purpose you will prepare and structure your presentation differently. You may use props instead of handouts. You may dress differently. Your purpose is to speak but entertain.

Educate

If you have been asked to *educate* your audience, this means to inform, to provide important information. This could be product knowledge, theory, teaching a new skill, or presenting research and statistics. Your audience wants to leave with information they did not have prior to the presentation. The information will make a difference to them. You may be the expert in your field delivering this important information or the educator/trainer in a classroom.

Persuade Into Action

Perhaps you have been asked to speak because you inspire people and you can sell the benefits of a product or service effectively. Your purpose may be to *persuade into action*. This could mean implementing a new strategy at work, it could be convincing a company to explore doing business with your company for the first time, or it could be selling a marketing idea. Your main purpose is not to entertain or even to educate. Although both of these may not be excluded from your presentation, your main purpose is to persuade the audience into an action.

Ceremonial

One of the most common types of speeches is the ceremonial speech, a speech at a wedding, a funeral, a school graduation or at the mother-in-law's 60th birthday party.

What type of speech will you prepare for these occasions? A speech with lots of human stories. Human stories about the person being spoken about or stories about the particular audience. If you are known in your family or business circle as a good speaker, don't be surprised if you find yourself doing many ceremonial speeches.

Every presentation may incorporate more than one of these purposes and some may include all of them, but which one is your main purpose? Once you understand the main purpose it makes the planning process much easier.

Resister, Supporter, Enthusiast

So, you have been asked to speak – or did you ask someone for the opportunity to speak?

There are three types of people when it comes to speaking: Those who *resist* the opportunity, those who *support* the opportunity and those who are *enthusiastic* and seek opportunities.

The Resister

When asked to speak or present, is your first thought, "Kill me now" or your second thought, "I'm sure Bill would love to embrace the challenge. I'll go and find him immediately"? Resisters will usually do anything to get out of being the speaker. They will come up with 101 excuses from the poor dead dog to having to leave the country in an emergency, or the laryngitis that developed out of nowhere on the morning of the presentation.

Resisters type A have no intention of ever overcoming the fear of public speaking. Their attitude could be, "I will never speak in public so I will never see the point in learning how to do it or facing my fear... so let's talk about something else... "

Or you could be the *Resister type B* who resists every opportunity, but you would still like to develop the skills and overcome the fear so you can become a Supporter or even an Enthusiast. The fact that you are reading this book confirms you are not a Resister type A. By the last page of the book I am aiming for no more Resisters. Resister A would not even be reading a book of this nature unless they were really a closet Resister type B.

The Supporter

This type of speaker supports the fact that they may have to speak to achieve an outcome. They may even be speaking on a regular basis. They may or may not enjoy it. They accept it as part of their job role or life. They may not go and look for opportunities but they certainly do not resist opportunities. They support the benefits of speaking and presenting. The Supporter will also accept that their skill needs to be developed and improved and the better the skill the better the outcome. Some Supporters wonder what all the fuss is about. They may still get nervous and suffer from the same levels of anxiety before a big presentation, but they accept it is part of the process and they do it anyway. They will also support other friends, colleagues or staff by acknowledging that these essential skills may help others achieve success.

The Enthusiast

Yes this is me. The Enthusiast is usually employed in a job that requires a lot of speaking. They have deliberately studied, or put themselves in a position where speaking is a part of their life. They could be a teacher, a trainer, a professional speaker, a radio personality or even a salesperson who loves people interaction. Not all these professions are necessarily made up of speaking Enthusiasts. A teacher's main purpose could be to make a difference and they accept that they have to speak to reach the outcome. You can probably think of many more careers for this type of speaker. Some Enthusiasts are not in careers where they have the opportunity to speak so they may become members of organisations like Toastmasters or National Speakers, they may join networking groups or even a theatre group that gives them any opportunity to speak and perform.

It doesn't matter which category you fall into. It doesn't mean that the Enthusiast is naturally a better speaker or presenter. It usually means that because they look for opportunities, they have had much more practice than others and have probably spent a considerable amount of time developing their skill and style.

The Message

At the end of the day it does not really matter to the audience or the person who asked you to speak, whether you are an Educator, an Entertainer, a person who has tried everything to get out of delivering the presentation or a person who has raced to the podium.

The only thing that matters, the one important essential ingredient in every presentation, is The Message.

If you have nothing to say, stop talking. If you have nothing to say, get away from the spotlight.

Your message is everything. Answer these key questions:

- What is the one message that I want everyone in this room to remember when the presentation is over?

- Why am I the one to be here to present this information?

- What have the audience come here for?

- What is the action that needs to occur when the presentation is over?

- What message have I been asked to communicate to the audience?

Even if your main purpose is to entertain there will still be a Key Message for the audience.

When we work on your structure we will explore Key Messages in more detail so you can ensure the message you have come to share with the audience is the message they take home.

You may know now that you are a Supporter of speaking; you may know that you need to leave your audience with a message and you may even understand your purpose and have decided that for most of your presentations you are there to educate and inform.

Even if you have all your ducks lined up there is still something that lurks inside all of us. It creates barriers to success. It stops us from standing up and stepping forward. Fear and speaking nerves.

Turn the pages to explore why we fear speaking and how we can learn to overcome anxiety and use nerves positively.

Security is mostly a superstition. It does not exist in nature.
Life is either a daring adventure or nothing

Helen Keller

3. SHAKIN' IN YOUR BOOTS

Before you come to the conclusion that you are the only person who is truly terrified of public speaking – you are not alone. Even the most professional speaker will still have feelings of butterflies and anxiety before a presentation. What counts is what we do with those nerves.

Speaking in public (depending on the particular study, and there have been so many) rates in our top four fears – a higher fear than death in most research. As Jerry Seinfield put it so eloquently, it means that at a funeral you would rather be the one in the casket than the one reading the eulogy.

Do you have a fear or do you have a phobia?

A phobia is described in the Collins Dictionary as: *an irrational, persistent fear of something or a situation.*

Perhaps we could describe it as Public Speaking Phobia because if you really think about it and analyse your fear it could be seen to be a little *irrational.* I don't think anyone has actually died while giving a speech, even if you swear it feels like you could have a heart attack.

So What Are Nerves?

Nerves are fear. Most people believe they need to overcome nerves.

You actually need to understand your fear and then develop strategies to not let fear overtake you.

- Do your nerves prevent you from reaching your potential?
- Do your public speaking nerves interfere with promotional opportunities?
- Does your fear of public speaking make you feel inadequate and lacking in self-esteem?
- Does your fear stand in the way of meeting new people and making important contacts?
- Does your fear stop you from attending functions that may require you to speak?

If you have answered "yes" to any of these I am glad you have decided to pick up Speaking in the Shower and are choosing steps to overcome your fear and develop your presentation skills.

So what happens physically to our bodies when we experience fear?

- Increased heart rate
- Sweating
- Headaches
- Shortness of breath
- Shaking, tremors or twitching
- Overwhelming irrational thoughts of danger and consequences
- Loose bowel movements
- Muscle tenseness
- Dizziness
- Insomnia
- Dry mouth

Sometimes what is happening to our bodies when we experience fear is worse than the fear itself.

In 1915 Walter Connon coined the "Fight or Flight" theory to describe how an animal reacts to threats. We as humans also react with the Fight or Flight response. When faced with a threat or fear we can stay and fight or we can run. It has also been referred to as "Fight, Flight or Freeze". We can all relate to this with regards to public speaking. Do you fight and face the fear? Is your first reaction to run? Or do you freeze?

How do we get over fear? Do you just read through this book, pick up a few tips and you are cured? Unfortunately it's not as easy as that. However, you can start to understand your fear and then, along with some suggestions and tips from either this book or a Speaking in the Shower workshop, you are on your way to developing some workable strategies to stand up and speak out and have the skills to steer your fear into workable energy.

Let's Work With The Idea Of Consequence

Nerves = Fear

Fear = Consequence

What Will Happen If...?

If I have a fear of flying...

What are the worst possible consequences if I fly? Okay, pretty bad consequence with that one.

What is the best case scenario? The flight feeds me, pampers me and somehow the plane lands on a tropical island and we are deserted with all our favourite people and the airline also pays me lots of money for the terrible inconvenience.

And what is the most probable? I fly, I have a pleasant flight with no real adventures and I land at my destination and continue with my life.

Okay, let's look at delivering a speech at work:

The worst case scenario: I forget what I am saying (I am not prepared). The staff do not like what I am proposing (I can listen to them). I am sweating and my heart is pounding (take a little quiet time prior to the meeting and wear lightweight clothes). I forget 40% of the presentation (did you remember the key points?? The rest can be sent in a memo). I look like a fool because I am stuttering and can't get my words out (probably everyone in the room already knows you are a competent individual and someone else may help you along). You have just made a huge error in judgement by shouting at everyone in the audience and telling them they are all idiots (apologise and explain that you felt a bit under pressure and were having trouble getting your message across). Generally all is forgotten in a very short period of time.

15

Best case scenario: Everyone in the room thinks you are awesome. You remember every word of your one-hour presentation and persuade every person in the room into action immediately. Then all attendees spend the next hour telling you about your superb public speaking skills and invite you to be the speaker at the next management function. (You just never know – this could happen.)

Most probable scenario: You are feeling anxious prior to the presentation (you take a quiet time beforehand to get everything organised). You prepare well and you have a great structure that you follow to the end. Your main points are communicated and you have a few handouts for everyone to take with them. The short DVD you show really demonstrates the point. Everyone leaves with the outcome of the presentation achieved.

And a presentation for a large group:

Worst case scenario: Doesn't go according to plan, data projector won't work and you can't remember the presentation without the slides. Instead of a one-hour presentation it is all over in 16 minutes and everyone goes to lunch early. You think a couple of the key points got through but can't be sure.

Best case: You can let your mind wander with the best case so let's go straight to the most probable.

Most probable: You get there in plenty of time to prepare the room, meet organisers of the event and have a chance to meet some of the audience. You collect a couple of business cards from keen people wishing to speak to you after the event. The data projector isn't connected correctly when you arrive but this is rectified and a test run is organised while you are setting up. The presentation goes exactly as you prepared. There are a few great questions that you answer well and one difficult question that you say you will find out the answer to and get back to the audience member shortly. You close the presentation with a powerful message and the intended outcome is achieved. Looking back at the feedback reports all participants state that it met their expectations and they think the presenter is well organised, professional and an expert in their field.

Although a long-winded way to get to my point across, my message to you is that the presenter was not subjected to hours of horrific torment.

If you look at the worst case scenario and discover that it is not so bad after all and it will not change your life as you know it, it may just give you the confidence to take the big step, risk it, feel the fear and do it anyway, as the best case and most probable scenarios are definitely worth the risk.

Tips From A Four-Year-Old

For the past 20 years I have been teaching kids to speak from three years old right through to the big kids – the "big kids" were about 63 years old. The "consequence factor" was more evident the older they were.

A three or four-year-old speaking on the microphone about their favourite dolly was having a lovely chat to their classmates. There was no fear, only excitement about who was going to go first. The microphone was seen as a fun toy and the experience was rewarded with questions from an eager audience wanting to know why dolly's hair has been cut, and praise from their teacher – that was me – for having their turn and speaking in such a lovely voice.

The six to eight-year-olds were similar but a small number seemed to be a bit nervous. When students were asked to explain their nerves they said it was usually because they were starting to compare themselves with others in the class and may not seem as good as them on the microphone. Or, if they were talking about what they did on the weekend, their story may not have been as exciting as their classmates. But still, with some encouragement, all kids in this age group supported the speaking we did each week and, without too much coaxing, learnt to enjoy it and looked for opportunities to use their skill – such as volunteering to speak at their performances and parent nights.

Nine- to twelve-year-olds were just starting to understand what the consequence would be of not doing (what they interpreted as) a great job speaking in front of an audience. They may look silly... What if they forget what they are meant to be saying? Many of the physical symptoms of nerves were starting to show, especially if they were preparing a speech for another day rather than an impromptu discussion on what they did on the holidays.

Again, with coaching and support and some education about speaking, this age group were still keen to try their skill, take the risk and reap the rewards.

The young teens of 13 to 17 years were all about what everybody else was thinking about them. Will the others mock me at school even if I do a great job? It wasn't so much about the content, it was all about the self-esteem, being ridiculed, their credibility in their social circle being damaged. It was a very rare occasion if any of them refused to speak but they were much more particular about who was going to be there, who else was going to be speaking, and what they were going to wear. It was with this age group I delivered much personal development and life skill training. I promoted exceptional communication skills and how to speak to an audience as a great asset. A skill to be valued. The fear and anxiety was starting to creep in at this age as they were much more aware of the consequences of their actions.

The adults who enrolled in my courses were the biggest surprise. Very early on in my career, I asked a quiet, well groomed young lady on her first class to hop up to the microphone to tell everyone a little bit about herself and why she had enrolled in the course.

There were 12 in the class and she was the second to last to present her information. Everyone took approximately one minute to present, so this young lady spent 15 minutes thinking about her one-minute presentation. Instead of thinking about what she was going to say, she started to think about all the things that could go wrong. What if she couldn't adjust the microphone to her height, what if she couldn't speak loud enough, what if she looked like an idiot in front of all these other confident class members? And on it went. The anxiety got so bad that when she walked up to have her turn, she stood in front of the microphone and burst into tears. When giving her a comforting hug she was physically shaking. Her physical appearance gave me no indication of the extent of her fear when I announced her.

Over the next few weeks, along with the support of her classmates, she spoke on the microphone and, at the end-of-year performance, introduced herself and welcomed the audience to her graduation, in front of 800 people. We worked on strategies to work with the fear and self-talk, not the phobia of public speaking.

So what are your worst fears about speaking in public?

Do they seem rational or not? Do you try hard to justify your fears to yourself and others around you?

Turn Your Nerves Into Positive Energy

Let's acknowledge that we all have nerves to some extent. How do we work with them instead of nerves being our enemy? How do you turn total anxiety into exhilaration?

In 1975 Hans Selye published a model dividing stress into "Eustress" and "Distress".

He describes the bad stress as Distress – a harmful stimuli that makes you weaker, less confident and less able. Definitely describes an extremely anxious speaker.

Then there is Eustress – a healthy, normal stress that we use positively to reach for goals, to challenge ourselves and to feel good.

Eu is a Greek prefix for "healthy" or "all that is good". It is used in the same sense in the word *euphoria*. Think of the physical stress of losing weight but the feeling we get after a run or a workout; for those of you who have skied, the nerves standing at the top of a mountain, feeling the fear, doing it anyway and the euphoria you feel at the bottom of the run. Even giving birth for the first time – the sheer terror of the unknown and the thought of pain and all that can go wrong, and then the ultimate euphoria when your baby is born and placed in your arms.

Now think about the same concept with speaking.

Distress – all those physical symptoms you may feel beforehand. The panic, the anxiety, the fear.

Now attempt to turn that into Eustress and then imagine the euphoria at the finish line of a great presentation.

Turn your self-talk into positive talk. Take on the Eustress not the Distress.

Self-Talk – Mind Over Matter

Imagine you have just walked onto the stage. Five hundred wide eyes are looking at you as you take your place behind the lectern.

Self-talker 1 – We'll call him Bob

Oh my, what have I done, look at all those people staring at me. What if I can't remember the opening? I'm going to look like an imbecile. That bald man in the front row looks like he is angry already. I can feel my armpits starting, I knew I shouldn't have worn purple, the sweat marks are going to show through. The last speaker was fantastic, how can I possibly compete with that? I've been introduced... I feel like I'm going to vomit.

Self-talker 2 – Introducing Bill

Wow, what a big audience. How lucky am I to have this opportunity to share this new information with so many people?! I am feeling a little nervous... who wouldn't, I guess? I am so prepared though – everything is in its place and I know this information I am sharing today will have a positive impact on everyone in this room. I hope I get a chance to answer questions and meet some of the audience after the event. That bald man in the front row looks very curious about what I am here for, hopefully I can knock his socks off with this great new research. Oh that's my cue... I'm on.

Are you Bob or Bill? Of course you may wish to be Bobbette or Billette.

How is your self-talk?

It is a bit like, "Is the glass half empty or half full?" Do you complain that the rose bush has prickles or rejoice in the brilliance of a perfect rose?

Facing any fear has to start with you – with your mind and how you perceive the fear and what reward you will receive by facing your fear and doing it anyway.

So let's re-cap this chapter:

Nerves = Fear

Fear = Consequences (visit the consequences. Look at the worst case, best case and most probable outcome)

Distress = Harmful stimuli

Eustress = Healthy stress

Negative talk = Go back to nerves and start again

Positive talk = Turn your nerves into positive energy and go for it

Euphoria = The ultimate feeling after a presentation

The older we get, the more anxious, fearful and nervous we can feel.

So take a tip from a four-year-old and get excited about the next time you get the opportunity to show and tell. Use all your nervous energy to speak from the heart and be passionate about your message.

Your imagination is your preview of life's coming attractions

Albert Einstein

4. I HAVE ACCEPTED THE CHALLENGE – NOW WHAT?

Well done, we are moving into the zone of being a Supporter. You have accepted, or you are considering accepting, the challenge of speaking in public.

Preparation, Preparation, Preparation

In real estate, it's location, location, location. In presentations and speaking, it's preparation, preparation, preparation. It is said that for every hour of a presentation there are seven hours preparation. From the content you will be delivering, to accessing the right resources, knowing who you will be delivering to and even preparing the perfect outfit for the occasion, all comes down to perfect planning.

Being prepared can alleviate stress and nerves by at least 50%.

Many presenters just ensure their content is right and leave everything else to the organisers or chance. Then, when things go wrong, the presenter can look more incompetent than the organisers even if it was not the presenter's fault.

On the other hand, when the projector blows up and you can move onto flip charts, notes and audience activities and still manage to give a great presentation, the organisers will be thankful to you and the audience will be impressed with your calm demeanour and professionalism in a crisis.

All of these vital ingredients will be explained as you read through the following chapters.

Now we are going to get down to preparing your perfect, professional presentation.

Your Structure

In the next chapter we will be looking at how to structure your presentation with the Seven Steps to Presentation Success. But there is preparation before you get on to the actual structure.

Your Purpose

So, remember from chapter 1: What is your purpose? Is it to Entertain, to Educate, to Persuade the Audience into Action or is it a Ceremonial Speech? Or is it a combination? If it is a combination, what percentage is in each category? It could be:

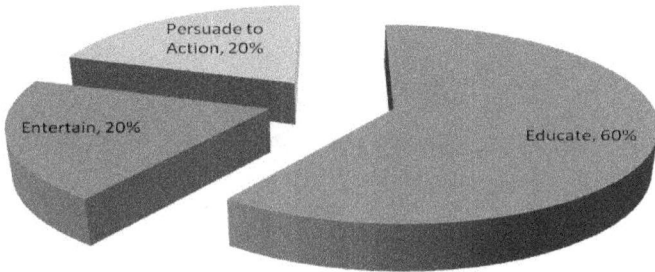

Persuade to Action, 20%
Entertain, 20%
Educate, 60%

Or it could be:

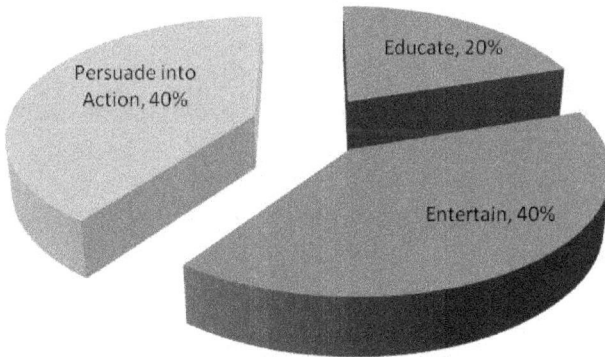

Persuade into Action, 40%
Educate, 20%
Entertain, 40%

Once you have your purpose you will become much clearer on how to get your message across.

Your Message

This is the critical element in any presentation. I will say it again – *critical*.

The message is why you are there in the first place. If you had nothing to say you would not be making a presentation or you would be there just wasting your time and everyone else's.

The message is *what* you have come to say, not *how* you are going to say it.

For example:

> *We need to increase our sales by 50% within the next six months or we are not going to survive.*

Or

> *When you leave today you will need to remember these three important points:*
>
> o   *First impressions do count*
>
> o   *Dress for success*
>
> o   *You need to manage your professional image.*

Or

> *Our customers are the reason we are moving to the new system.*

Or

> *Customers have told us what we need to do better.*

When starting to prepare for your presentation, be very clear about your message. You may have been asked to be a guest speaker for an organisation or you could have been asked to address a meeting. The first thing you need to ask is: "What is the message you want me to give to the audience?"

Others may describe it as: "What is the outcome you wish to achieve? What is the moral of the story?"

Whatever you wish to call it, the only reason you are standing there talking is because you have a message.

If your purpose is to entertain, there will still be a message in there for you to get out and share. You may be talking for an hour about your journey as a sports star, entertaining the crowd with your hilarious stories and real life dramas, but there will still be a message for your audience. The message could be: Work together as a team for success; or: Never give up when times are tough.

When we look at the structure I will give you suggestions and strategies on how, when and where to put your message.

Choosing A Method Of Delivery

So, you know that your purpose is to educate your audience about our new customer service survey results and you know you want to persuade the team into changing our current system to enable us to more effectively meet our customers' needs.

You know the message:

Our customers are the reason we are moving to the new system

Customers have told us what we need to do better.

So what is the best possible way to present this to the audience? How do you engage the audience? If they are engaged they are more likely to learn.

There are methods of delivery appropriate for small numbers of participants, there are the best methods for teaching people a skill, there are methods used to persuade people into action. There are so many to choose from... So how do you choose?

Remember the Chinese proverb:

I hear and I will forget

I see, I may remember

Involve me and I will understand

Do you want to involve your audience so they will understand the information? In his book How to Develop and Present Staff Training Courses, Peter Sheal discusses the research on how much we take in from different methodologies. Peter states that we tend to remember:

10% of what we read

20% of what we hear

30% of what we see

50% of what we see and hear

70% of what we say

90% of what we both say and do

So what does that mean to you, the presenter, if you have a two-hour presentation, where all you are doing is talking to the audience and giving them facts and figures? When the audience leaves they will probably only remember about 20% of the entire presentation and that's only if you do it well and can engage them for that long. Not good at all, especially for the person paying you – and that could also be the audience if they are the paying customers.

So what does 10% of what we read mean? That is the presenter giving the audience a text book and statistics from the survey and asking them to read through the information.

What about 20% of what we hear? Well that is you telling them about it.

30% of what we see? This could be a PowerPoint presentation with the statistics in a chart and some photos of the customers or the sales team in action.

50% of what we hear and see? You the presenter speaking about the survey, presenting facts perhaps in the form of a PowerPoint presentation or drawing a graph on a flip chart, then showing a short video of what happens in one of the stores.

If you were in the audience, do you think you will be starting to get some of the message?

70% of what we say? That means getting the audience to talk about it. That could be in a group discussion after they have watched some or all of the presentation, participating in a role-play (pick your audience for a role-play). It could be the audience making a presentation about it to the other groups.

And of course the last one: 90% of what we say and do. Use as many of the above strategies as possible. And the ultimate learning experience is when they actually have a chance to do the real thing.

Of course sometimes when delivering a presentation they may not have the chance to do the real thing – but it could be a simulation, or on your powerful closing in your presentation you could be persuading the audience into action so they go and experience the real thing.

Keep the research in mind when planning your presentation. Choose an effective combination so your audience will remember your key message and the learning experience.

These percentages of course may vary for each individual. If a person is a big reader their learning preference may be a little more text than an audience member who is more of a visual learner.

So now you may be thinking, a bit of talk, a bit of a slide show, get the audience to have a small group discussion, then it will all work out.

For many presentations this could be the perfect formula. But see below a few more suggestions of methods to get your message across.

Standard Presentation – You are the main resource and you will be speaking to the audience with or without additional resources for approximately 70% of the presentation.

Workshop – Participants are active.

Seminar – Group of people coming together to discuss a topic.

Conference – A formal get together to discuss/learn about important topics.

Group Discussion – Small groups discuss a topic or an issue.

Audience Activity – In small groups or as a large group, a planned activity that involves the audience for a deeper level of learning.

Games – Games are great, but not great without a purpose. Choose a game that is clearly linked to an outcome. A game of building the highest tower out of playing cards could be aligned with understanding team dynamics.

Brainstorming – An unfiltered method of getting the audience to give opinions, solutions and ideas before any reasoning and analysing is done.

Clinics – A group activity where you give the group a problem, they then diagnose and provide a solution or a cure. Great for several groups to participate to demonstrate there are always many solutions to problems.

Field Trips, Excursions – Seeing real things or people in action.

Demonstrations – Where your participants actually get to see the real thing or a simulation.

Technology Presentations – Besides the data projector, there are so many different types of technology that we can use in our presentations. Like a tablet which enables you to draw pictures and as you draw, it is projected on the big screen. Or webinars, a seminar online, or you can even survey your audience using pads or their mobile phones and the audience statistics are imported directly onto the big screen as they are entering the information. Of course by the time this book is released another five forms of presentation technology will be in the process of being developed. As a presenter or a speaker, try very hard to be up to date with technology even though it is difficult. It will do wonders for your credibility if used appropriately.

Using DVDs and other video recordings – Great for visuals. Look into appropriate copyright first to ensure you are legally allowed to use it.

Keynotes – You are the key speaker or one of the key speakers at an event. This may be a 15-minute slot or an hour. Be careful not to use so many methods that your keynote may appear rushed. The audience has come to see you as the main speaker. Ensure you are the main resource.

Question and Answer Sessions – Some presentations are based on a short presentation then the main purpose is to answer the questions of the audience members. This could also be described as a panel presentation or discussion.

There are many other training and teaching methods for classroom instruction or skill attainment but the delivery methods above will give you a guide to some methods you can use in your presentations and training sessions.

What About The Audience?

Who is in the audience?? It is essential you know this at the preparation stage. This will have an impact on how you prepare each time. For every audience your purpose, message and choice of delivery method may change even if the topic is the same.

You wouldn't deliver the same presentation to a small group of senior managers the same way you would deliver to a group of 17-year-olds also wanting to learn about how to work in teams more effectively, or how to implement technology into your workplaces. The Gen Y team could want a pretty fast-paced interactive session where perhaps some of the more mature members or others who have not embraced technology would want something a little slower.

Find out about your audience as soon as humanly possible.

- Who are they?
- What are their expectations?
- What is the age group?
- What are their roles?
- Are there more males than females?
- Do they go to similar presentations on a regular basis?
- Are they supportive and eager about the presentation?
- What is their prior knowledge?

Over the last four decades there have been many studies on learning preferences and personality styles. The need to demonstrate a learner-centred approach to learning is now not only accepted but expected within our classrooms and learning environments.

One of the most common and widely used theories over the years has been Neil Fleming's VARK model:

- **V**isual learners
- **A**uditory learners
- **R**eading/writing-preference learners
- **K**inaesthetic learners or tactile learners

Honey and Mumford's Learning Preference research (1982 and 1983) suggests that we are divided into four types of learners.

The Activist: The type who love to get up and go and participate in active learning. They involve themselves fully without bias to new experiences.

The Pragmatist: They are keen on trying new ideas, theories and techniques; the people who come back from management meetings excited about putting it all into practice.

The Reflector: They like to stand back and observe from many perspectives. They think "look before you leap". Not a good idea to start your presentation with a group charade activity with the Reflectors.

The Theorist: They like to analyse and synthesise, they will be the ones to question "Does this all make sense?" They want proof before they implement new ideas.

So, you are about to step up to the platform for the big speak and you announce to the audience within the first few minutes that they will all be participating in a few role-plays today. Your audience members are mainly Theorists who work as academics at the local university. The group is seeking new research and statistics to include in their class manuals.

Puzzled, at the end of a really hard day, you ask yourself, "Why did this exact same presentation really hit the mark with the theme park operators last week?"

Know your audience.

Although it may be impossible on most occasions to find out the personality or learning preference of every individual in the room, you can find out a little by asking their supervisors or the participants in pre-presentation communication. Or, what some experienced presenters do, is ask a few general questions to the audience at the beginning of their presentation like:

Who loves to lead a team rather than be one of the team?

Who loves to research new theories before putting them into practice?

Who here is a list person and just can't go to sleep until the list is done?

Who would get really nervous if you had to make a decision right now without any time to think about all the facts, figures and consequences of the decision?

Or you may just ask one question when the music fills the room.

Show of hands right now. Who wants to get up and boogie?

Sometimes with a few general questions you can gauge the type of audience you have and you can adapt a few group activities or offer to send out more research on the topic after the presentation concludes.

Having an understanding that different learning preferences do exist makes you much more aware of how you can cater for all types even in a relatively small presentation.

Get them involved, provide some form of text or resource for further information gathering, give them challenges and ensure you leave time for the Reflectors to think about your theories and suggestions before making them commit to action or even answer one of your questions.

One of the hardest things to do – but the most powerful – is getting the audience on your side. Actively accommodating a range of personality types and learning preferences is a success strategy used by many a speaking professional.

It is also great to know what style or personality type you are.

I am an Activist/Pragmatist. So if I do not cater for different learning preferences in my sessions, I may decide to start with charades at 9am in the morning and plan a fun-filled day full of hands-on activities and role-play. I would exhaust many learners and also risk alienating half my audience who don't want to tap dance around the conference floor.

If you understand yourself, you know where your strengths lie – and you will also know the areas to develop to ensure you don't just plan your presentations around how you would like it done.

As you can see there is a lot involved in preparing your presentation. Once you have your message, your purpose, your target audience and the method of delivery you now have to put it all together in a structure that will wow your audience every time.

5. SEVEN STEPS TO PRESENTATION SUCCESS

We have talked about Preparation, Preparation, Preparation which is all well and good. There are a lot of speakers who spend hours, days, even weeks preparing for their presentation. It helps if you know what to prepare, how to prepare and now how to structure your presentation.

If you don't put all the stuff in the right place then it will only ever be stuff. Stuff that you said that no one will really remember anyway.

The way you structure your presentation is an essential part of the planning process. It is how you put all the pieces of the jigsaw puzzle together to finish with the big picture. The big picture (your message) is what the audience should remember when they leave.

Let me introduce you to the model of the Seven Steps to Presentation Success which I have developed and used over the many years I have been presenting.

Step 1 Guess What?

(Get attention and incite curiosity)

Step 2 Why Me?
(This is who I am, this is why I am here. Credibility statement)

Step 3 Why You?
(This is all about your audience – this is how I can help you. Key Message)

Step 4 The Destination
(This is where we are going and how we are going to get there)

Step 5 The Journey
(The information you are going to share with the audience)

Step 6 The Relationship
(I am interested in you, what else can I do for you?)

Step 7 The Arrival
(Action, Key Message, Powerful close)

Let us explore each step in detail so you can start planning your dynamite presentation.

Step 1. Guess What?

When you are standing there in front of your audience and are waiting to start and you have 100 people talking, moving their chairs around, switching off their phones and introducing themselves to the person in the row in front of them, do you really want to start with your big opening story and have most of the room miss it?

Your opening in a presentation is as powerful as your closing. You want everyone in the room to have all eyes and ears on you. You want the audience to be ready to receive the information, to be informed, to be entertained, to be ready for YOU.

You need to get their attention and incite curiosity. And the best thing about this part is there are literally thousands of ways you can do this.

Let's look at a few examples.

The lights go out in the auditorium, the loud music starts to play and a voiceover is heard introducing the event and the speaker as the lights slowly come up and you are standing in the middle of the stage ready for your audience.

Yes, quite dramatic but hey, they are ready for you.

You may not be on a stage, you may be in a boardroom or in a classroom and don't have the big stage crew on hand. So you may just start with a question to the audience or a powerful statement. For example, you have 50 people in a sales meeting and your question is: "Who would like to increase their sales by 100% by the end of this month?"

Or a statement: "Our brand will cease to exist forever by Friday..."

The people in that room want to listen now, you have their interest and they want more.

Music is also a powerful thing. You have 20 or 30 people in the room all born in the 70s or 80s. Start the session with a music piece and ask the audience who the artist is and when it was released, and then another. Then make the piece relevant to the topic you are going to be talking about.

Or you may just stand there and do or say nothing for a long period of time holding an unusual prop until everyone is looking at you. Then just say "Hi..."

Or you can say and do absolutely nothing and put a visual up on the big screen. A picture says a thousand words. You could put up a photograph of a person in a suit behind bars if you were talking to a group about fraud and dishonest practices. Or, for the work/ life balance talk, a picture of yourself in a deckchair on the beach sipping a cocktail.

Sometimes someone else will do the attention grabbing for you like your announcer.

Know who your audience is first and then decide what would incite their curiosity, what will get their attention, then figure out an interesting and unique way of doing it.

Step 2. Why Me?

This is a story about why you are there talking to them. Who are you and what do you have to offer?

The audience will want to know why they are spending time listening to you. This is your credibility statement or story. Your credibility is an important aspect of your presentation.

- ✔ You want them to believe you.
- ✔ You want them to trust you.
- ✔ You want them to listen to any advice.
- ✔ You want them to take action based on your action or words.
- ✔ You want them to like you.
- ✔ You want them to respect you.

This part of the structure is not always done by you. If you have to do it then this is where it fits. If it is not you, it will be the person who introduces you (if you are at a conference or seminar) and they may cover most aspects of a credibility statement.

Another strategy is to send attendees information about the presenter in a presentation flyer. If this is the case, don't give all the information – leave some surprises for the audience.

If someone else is introducing you, always write your own introductions. It is amazing how things get "lost in translation" or the MC misses out the most important qualification that gives you the right to the title of industry expert.

If you write your own introduction, you are the one who has control over what the audience listens to and what other information you may want to weave into your presentation.

Remember why you are there. If your purpose is to entertain a group of aged care workers at their end of year dinner, does it matter in your introduction that you have a double degree in economics?

If you are there to inform or educate, the audience will probably be looking for an industry or topic expert so include information that validates this for them.

If you are there to move people into action or to persuade, it may be your life story or an incident that happened to you or your passion on a topic that gives you credibility in the eyes of the audience.

You may use a little of each in your introduction but make it relevant to the presentation and the people.

Remember your audience and customise your introduction to suit. A "Why Me" story gives you credibility with *this* group, not last week's group in another country.

A lot of speakers find it hard to stand up and speak about their own achievements and accomplishments but you need to let your audience know why you are here. If you do struggle with telling your audience about yourself and your five bestselling books then ask someone else to do it for you, or give people the information, but don't ever miss it out.

You will find if you do not establish credibility, your audience will spend a substantial amount of time trying to figure it out instead of being engaged by your message.

Above all be authentic from the start. Your introduction will reveal to the audience a lot about you and about your reason for being there too.

An example of a short introduction could be:

> *As a winner of the prestigious small business award for 2009, it is my privilege and honour to share my story with you tonight. As a young person in business working hard to compete with people twice my age with twice my experience this award has helped me redefine my goals and direction. I hope my story will inspire you to keep going and work towards your dreams too.*

Or

> *I had been selling property for a little under five years when I came across a crazy idea. This crazy idea I tried and tested for three years with unbelievable results. My system has now been implemented in 230 real estate offices across the country which has the potential to change the way people buy houses.*

Some of course are much longer depending on the style of the presentation and how long you will be speaking for. If you are speaking for 20 minutes you can't spend – and the audience will not appreciate – five minutes of that time talking about yourself just to gain your credibility.

However, if you are training a group for a day or over a longer period of time then much more detailed information could be given. Remember, some can also be weaved through your presentation – case studies you have been involved in or your personal stories can be introduced along the presentation journey.

Your statement must never be your CV. You are not applying for a job, it is a different sort of selling yourself. There is nothing worse than a speaker saying "...then in1984 I changed jobs for three months, then in December 1985 I moved to..." etc.

The Why Me? part of your presentation is a story about the presenter and why you have been invited to speak or why you have asked for their time.

Step 3. Why You?

It is very rare for someone to come and hear you speak just to be nice to you or because they have nothing else to do (mums, kids, spouses and best friends excluded – they will come just because they are proud of you).

The audience wants something from you. They may not know what or why they want it yet but they instinctively know that if they come, if they listen, they will be rewarded. It's the WIIFM mindset. "What's In It For Me?" the audience wants to know.

- ✔ *Will this guy give me the information I want to enable me to do my work more efficiently?*

- ✔ *Can I use this information in my life to my advantage?*

- ✔ *What will this presentation do for me?*

- ✔ *Why am I here listening to this when I could be catching up with my work?*

- ✔ *What reward will I get for being here?*

Think about the last time you went to any presentation or listened to anyone speak. What questions did you ask yourself? What did you want from the presentation? They are all the same questions that your audience will be asking. So give them the answers before they ask. Tell them, WHY YOU?

In this part of the presentation you are providing the reasons for everyone being there. This is a critical part of your presentation to keep your audience engaged from the start. This is when your Key Message is introduced. This is the message that you want your audience to remember and to leave with.

For example:

I am going to share with you today:

- *Our new product*

- *How you are going to get it out there*

- *How we are going to build a household brand name*

In your credibility statement you may have mentioned that you have launched 46 products to the shelf successfully over the past two years.

Now you are going to tell the audience: "I will help you launch this product. I can help you learn about your new product, I can help you get it on the shelves and I can help you ensure it becomes a household brand name."

In this part of your presentation your focus is about your audience and what they want, what they need – and that what you have to offer will be a reward for them.

Another example is:

During the next 10 days I will work together with you to ensure you achieve your qualification by Christmas. Your qualification can open new doors for you next year and offer a future full of possibilities.

So everyone can look forward to [Key Messages]:

- *Working hard until Christmas*
- *Achieving your qualification*
- *New opportunities*

Your Key Messages do not have to be in a set of three but it is helpful to remember the Rule of Three, an English rule that suggests people tend to remember things in sets of three:

- Location, location, location – Real estate
- Slip, slop and slap – Skin cancer campaign
- Stop, look and listen – Safety

Even storytellers use the Rule of Three in their titles. The Three Musketeers, Three Little Pigs, Goldilocks and the Three Bears.

Or how about:

- Blood, sweat and tears
- I came, I saw, I conquered
- Mind, body and soul

People even say: "Things always happen in threes".

Speakers usually follow the Rule of Three as it is a rhythmic habit that the audience uses and will continue to use. So if you ask the audience what are the four Key Messages it will be much harder for them to remember all four than a rhythmic three.

Whenever you have been asked to speak, ask yourself "What do I want my audience to remember?" This is your Key Message.

Ensure it goes at the front of your presentation (you can also use a Key Message in your Guess What? if it is done in a powerful way) and always again at the end.

People will remember the first and last messages from a presentation, the first and last things they read, the first and last things they see.

Step 4. The Destination

This is when you tell the audience what to expect.

Sometimes you may choose to surprise your audience and not tell them exactly where they are going until they get there. But for many participants in a classroom or in an audience they like to know what will be happening over the next three hours.

It depends on the people in the audience but why choose to alienate anyone by not sharing a little information to help them relax and focus on the presentation?

Can you imagine if you were in the audience and you missed out on essential information because your mind was wandering, wondering when you could use the restrooms? Or you were getting hungry and had no idea when you would be taking a break. Or you were so confused about what direction the presentation was going in that you were not taking the appropriate notes.

If you can, let your audience know where you are going to take them and how.

Following on from your Key Message you can then say:

> *Over the next three hours I will be sharing with you some of the ideas I have presented to the other departments of our company, and their reactions.*
>
> *We will also have time to discuss some of those reactions in small groups.*
>
> *I will be handing out some of the findings from the research at the end of today so you can take it back to share with your colleagues.*
>
> *If I have not answered all of the questions by the end of the presentation Mr Jones will be hosting a panel Q and A after morning tea which I am sure will also be a great interactive discussion.*

Or something a little less formal:

> *Expect the unexpected today. Before the end of the day you may be moving out of your comfort zone just a little. Role-playing, debating, discussions, brainstorming and a little dancing is how we are going to learn about and experience customer satisfaction.*

Different approach but it gives people a sense of direction.

Some presenters will present a timetable or an agenda for the day. What do you think your audience will appreciate?

Take the guessing away without taking away all the surprises you have in store for them.

Step 5. The Journey

Well, we are finally here. The part where you actually get the chance to give the information to the audience. It could be the facts, the research, your stories, examples, new key information.

The nuts and bolts of your presentation are placed in this part of the structure. If the presentation is about an hour long this part will take up to about 40-45 minutes.

This is the part where you need to choose the appropriate delivery method, the best method of getting your message across.

It could be you presenting with the aid of a PowerPoint presentation. It could be group work or presenting case studies. You could be facilitating a game that teaches people how to work better in teams.

This is the part where you need to apply strategies to engage your audience to the end.

You have done the preparation.

You have their attention.

You have your credibility.

Your audience knows why they are there.

They know where they are going.

Now take them there – in an exciting, interesting, informative, entertaining and engaging ride – always keeping in mind the outcomes and the Key Message or messages you wish to leave your audience with.

This is the part that should flow quite easily for an industry or topic expert because this is the part you have been waiting for. Unfortunately, this is the part that some presenters start with. Then they can't quite figure out why it is not as successful as they thought it would be. The audience seems to be asking too many questions, is interrupting all the time or half the people in the room seem to be running off to the restrooms in the middle of vital statistics or, even worse, start asking for your credentials right when you are making a main point about research.

You need to set the scene, prepare the audience and let them know some of the ground rules without having to spell them out for them.

Then when it comes your time to be the expert, the entertainer, the influencer you will shine and the audience will open their eyes, ears and minds to you. And when you are also authentic and passionate about your presentation you will find they will open their hearts too.

Step 6. The Relationship

All business is about relationships. All communication is about relationships. Let there be no mistake about that.

Do you want to be a five-minute speaker who comes and goes, or do you want to build a relationship with your audience?

I hope you answered the latter.

A relationship can be described as a two way connection. When you are communicating with someone, you are wanting to connect with them. If you are on the platform talking to 300 people, you still want to connect with every individual if you can. You want to build a relationship with your audience as a whole and aim to make a connection with every individual.

But remember it is a two way street. You want to connect with your audience but they need to feel they can connect with you too. The best way to do this is by letting them know you care. You care about how this information will affect them, you care about how they can use the rewards of the presentation, and you are interested in them.

If you speak from the heart and share a piece or two of yourself with the audience they will start to connect with you. If you are genuinely interested in the people you are talking to, the audience will sense it.

Ways to show your audience that you are there to help them and want to build a relationship with them include:

- Promising to send them something and then actually doing it

- Thanking them for the opportunity to share your stories or information with them

- Offering to help them even more. This could be by getting an invitation to return to next year's conference with more research for them

- Joining them for lunch or refreshments after the presentation

- Offering them a gift like a free article or book

- Letting them know how they can contact you

- Researching their concerns or their achievements prior to the presentation and actually using them in your presentation

You also want to receive important feedback from your audience so you can evaluate your presentation and see what improvements can be made for next time. This can be done by asking participants to fill out a quick feedback form. More about evaluation and feedback later in the book.

A connection can happen in a few minutes, a relationship is built over time, a valued trust-based relationship is earned.

Step 7. The Arrival

This is the part of the presentation where you have to say goodbye and announce to the audience they have arrived at their destination.

Don't say "Thank you for allowing me to speak about my new vacuum cleaner" and leave the stage. Or say "What a great audience you have been, thank you for your time" and go home.

This part is the reason you are here. This is what you have been working towards with all your preparation and structuring and presenting.

This is your Powerful Close.

This is what your audience is leaving with – the last memorable action or words.

What will they be?

Of course... Your Key Message.

But before the last powerful words this is also a time when you want to influence the audience into action. You want them to reap their rewards from the presentation. Whoever asked you to speak wants a return on investment. You may want a return on investment too. So what do you want your audience to do?

- Use their time more effectively
- Buy what you are selling
- Change their way of answering the telephone
- Be more aware of diversity
- Implement a new system
- Find more time to spend with their families
- Go home and do their homework

If you want your audience to do something you need to ask them to do it.

You can set them a challenge, give them a mentor to work with, ask them to buy the book you have been talking about, ask them to answer the telephone in the new way and keep a record of comments for a week.

Whatever you would like them to do, whatever action you want them to commit to, ask them in this section.

Remember, if you have done everything right so far, the audience have connected with you and they want to take your advice. It may not be right now so don't always expect immediate action, it may be in a week or even a year.

The main point here is if you do not ask the audience to take action, to put into practice what they have learnt, many will go away with no goals or direction or any idea what they are meant to do with all this information.

Even an entertainer will have a message or an action for the audience; it may be as simple as to laugh more at work and use a new catchphrase.

So move your audience into action and then get ready to leave your platform with – you guessed it – the Key Message. If your message is the action you want them to perform then it is only one step and you have arrived.

Your Key Message may be aligned with the action but the three points, or two or even one, powerful message you want your audience to leave the room with, is the last thing you say.

It may not be word for word as in the introduction but the message has to be clear.

You now know all about our new product

Use the strategies we learnt today to get it onto the shelves

This product will be a household brand name by Christmas

Or the other scenario we used in our Why You?

Get your assignments into me as soon as you can

You will achieve your qualification this year if you put in the time

Then the doors will open with new opportunities

Your closing should be powerful. It is the message you came here to say.

So I know you may be thinking now "It all looks very complicated. It may take me an hour to get through the structure and I only have 20 minutes! What can I do?"

This structure can be used in a seven-day workshop or a two-minute presentation. Let me give you an example. See if you can see all seven steps in order in the presentation.

Who would like to own one million dollars worth of property by next year?

My name is Joanne Higgs and I was broke last year and struggling to pay my own electricity bill. I started to follow the ABC strategy and I now own one million dollars worth of property. I would like to share my story with you over the next 10 minutes so my story may help you achieve your financial goals too. The key to property success I found has been:

1. Location

2. A great relationship with my borrower, and

3. An open mind

[Then Joanne moves into her story for a few minutes.]

Thank you for inviting me here today to share my journey with you all. I would love to hear from you as you take your journeys so I will leave my details with Mr Jones and my cards are available at the back of the room.

Go home today and set a goal, then make a plan on how you are going to achieve it.

And remember, your key to success could be:

1. Location

2. The borrower

3. Your open mind

Look at the way you present or the way you train – are you using a structure?

You may be using a different structure that is working really well for you. The beauty about reading books like this and learning new ways is you get to choose what to take from it, you get to choose what is important for you, and how you personally can use it.

I encourage you to try the Seven Steps to Presentation Success structure to give you the confidence you need to stand up and say your message knowing you will look like a professional.

6. YOU ARE THE EXPERT IN BEING YOU

You have all seen or heard of a brilliant speaker, or you have listened to a speaker entertain the audience for hours on end with their funny jokes and stories, and watched them with awe. What about the trainer or teacher that everyone loves and their classrooms are full of laughter and filled with enthusiastic and engaged learners? Have you ever wanted to be just like them? Have you ever wanted to use their style and jokes and hoped you could also get the same response?

Well you can't. You know why? Because you are not them, you are you.

The best speakers in the world are the best because they don't try to be someone else, they are themselves. They may watch and learn from other people and look at some great ways they use the stage or the perfect timing in their presentation when they tell a story, but the story will always belong to them and no one will ever be able to tell it in the same way.

It is very hard to always be acting when you are speaking. It is hard to try to be someone you are not. You may fluke it occasionally but eventually people see straight through an act. The audience wants an authentic speaker who has the confidence to be themself.

The best thing is, you are already the expert in being you. There is no one else exactly the same. You are a unique speaker. When you speak about your life experiences and you tell a story, no one else can tell them like you do. They are your stories and your emotions when you tell them. You are already the expert in being you so you don't have to research the topic, back it up with statistical data and worry about the audience not agreeing with you.

"This is great!" you say. But who are you? Do you know what your strengths are? Do you know what you need to work on to make you more approachable so people can get to see who you are? Do you know and understand why you do the things you do in a presentation? Do you know what makes you unique?

Let's explore how you can be you and be a charismatic, confident speaker using your uniqueness and personality to stand out from the crowd.

Who Are You?

Why are you going to be speaking?

We have already discovered that you are speaking because you have a message to share. But let's get down to why you are the person who is saying the message from your perspective.

- Is it because someone sees you as a role model for others?

- Is it because you are a person who is passionate about a topic and wants to share that passion with others?

- Are you there because you feel you would like to make a difference to other people's lives?

- Are you there because it is your job and someone has to do it?

- Are you speaking because it is great for your ego and you enjoy the attention?

- Or are you really the industry expert?

- What intrinsic and extrinsic rewards are you receiving from speaking?

- Does it make you feel important, needed, valued, generous or some other emotion?

These are questions to ask yourself to find out a little more about who you are.

What Drives You? What Kind Of Learner Are You?

It helps to know what type of learner you are because this could influence how you present.

As I am an Activist and I know as a learner that I like to be involved in the process, I like group discussions and activities and anything to do with getting up and giving it a go. I could put together a presentation based on all the things I like because I think everyone in the room likes the same things or has the same learning preferences.

Getting to know who you are helps you to be a better presenter. Getting to know yourself also lets you see the great qualities that your audience loves about you and the not-so-good qualities, the ones that you need to work on or avoid altogether in a presentation.

One of the best ways to critique yourself is to record yourself. It can sometimes be quite confronting to watch yourself, so do it alone. Make a list of all the great things you are seeing and a list of the things that you didn't know you do. Lots of annoying habits are seen by others and never by yourself so watching them is the first step to acknowledging them and working on improving them.

I had a student in my class this year, training to be a presenter, who swayed from side to side through her whole presentation every time. We had discussed this and she thanked me for the feedback and her classmates gave her peer feedback and she thanked them for their feedback. But nothing changed.

The day she watched her 15-minute presentation on video playback was the day she made the commitment to change. She had no idea how distracting it was to her presentation and how she swayed for 15 minutes. She was amazed. Three weeks later, watching her present to a group, only a small sway was seen about five minutes into the presentation and that was all. Watching yourself is a powerful evaluation tool.

Comfortable and confident in your own skin is what you need to be. Comfortable and confident in how you will present.

Even though I encourage you to be you, there are still professional qualities that you will need to adopt and display for people to respect you and your message.

Below are seven characteristics of great public speakers:

Be Organised: Be organised not just on the day of your presentation but from the moment you have been invited to present. Your preparation will show before, during and after the presentation. Be organised with your follow-ups and feedback.

Be Authentic: That is the part about being you. Be genuine, be real and show integrity at all times.

Be Learning: Show your audience that you, just like them, are always learning and growing to be the best that you can be.

Be Passionate: Show energy and passion for your topic. Energy is contagious. If you are not excited and passionate about your topic don't expect your audience to be. Present with passion.

Be an Expert: Being an expert does not mean you have to know everything about your topic but you should know enough to give something to the audience. You may be a topic expert, but the reason you may be speaking rather than the industry expert is because you could be an expert in getting the audience to think more about the topic or to inspire them into action. You could be an expert in building teams, transferring a skill or the expert in sharing your stories like no one else can.

Be Respectful: Be respectful to everyone you come in contact with – the organisers, the catering staff, every member in the audience. Show everyone that, although you are there as the speaker or presenter, you value the input, values and opinions of others.

Have Heart and Soul: You are a real person. Show compassion, show emotions, connect with your audience. Be excited, be sad, be inspired.

Your Presentation Style

Are you softly spoken and sit down on a stool at the front of a classroom to tell your stories?

Are you gregarious and energetic and dance around the room?

Do you speak in perfect pitch and never use a word of slang?

Are you a big personality and can get away with some colourful and interesting use of the English language?

Are you a walking encyclopaedia who thrills the audience with your impromptu statistics and research when questions are received from the audience?

What type of presenter are you?

All great speakers will develop their own style. That is why in the first part of this chapter we talked about being you and finding out who you are, being comfortable and confident in your own skin.

When this happens you will start to develop your own style of presenting. This style will become part of your reputation as a speaker along with all the seven great characteristics.

My style for example is far from quiet. I tend to get a little excited along the way when I am speaking about something I am passionate about. If I were to ask any of my attendees to describe my style, they would say that I am energetic, dynamic and fun. Not all people would want to have an energetic speaker so they may choose to book someone else with a completely different style depending on what they are looking for.

A colleague of mine has a very different style to me and she would be described as the guru of her field and amazing to listen to. She isn't as energetic as me and she doesn't have to be. Her style is relaxed, informative, intense, and her stories are amazing to listen to. She is quietly spoken and still owns the room.

The first time I saw Glen Capelli, one of Australia's best speakers who is in constant demand as a speaker globally, I was in awe. Not straightaway – I had high expectations as I had heard of his reputation and couldn't wait to see him in action. For the first five minutes I thought, "This guy is pleasant to listen to, he seems professional and organised". It wasn't until two hours later, when I was still listening, enthralled, captivated, and it felt like I had been in the room 10 minutes not two hours, that I realised how powerful Mr Capelli was as a speaker. When we finally broke for lunch I wanted desperately to extend our session time, I wanted to listen to some more. So then the very next time he was in town, I was off to see him again – this time to analyse every step of his presentation. Guess what? Two hours later I was in the same spot, just enjoying and learning and growing. I forgot to analyse. Glen is inspiring, authentic, an expert in every topic he shares and has spent years developing his skill. You would never guess who I chose to be my coach and mentor.

Every speaker will have their own style, what works for them, what engages their audience, what connects them to their listeners. The last thing I want you to do is go out and try to emulate another speaker but do go and watch others in action, to learn and grow.

You don't have to go off to a conference to learn from speakers, it could be at a training course, a guest speaker at a school assembly, a person in a social setting telling a story that everyone seems to be engrossed in.

Great speakers are not always under the spotlight and on stage. They are people who have exceptional communication skills and will be comfortable in their own skins, being themselves.

If you have had the opportunity to speak on a few occasions, ask your colleagues, friends or attendees to describe your style. See if this is the same style you think you portray.

First Impressions And Your Professional Image

Being the director of a grooming and deportment school for nearly 20 years I cannot tell you how many times I have seen a teenager or a corporate miss out on a part-time after-school job or a professional appointment because of their professional image.

People are under the impression that your image is about the way you look, your personal presentation and what you wear. It is so much more than a designer suit and a fancy tie. Your professional image is a set of qualities and character traits that represent perceptions about your competence and character. Your professional image is an insight into who you are.

Whether you believe it to be right or wrong, people will judge you. People will make assumptions based on your:

Personal presentation – Your clothes, your hair, your shoes, your accessories

Personality – Can I work with this person? Do I like this person?

Actions – Did you promise to do something and did not deliver? Did you arrive on time?

Social skills – Did you introduce yourself? Are you displaying correct etiquette for the occasion? Are you treating others with respect?

Work ethic – Are you producing professional work? Are you putting in your very best?

When you are speaking or meeting someone for the first time, people will make assumptions within the first 30 seconds. That is generally how long it takes in a job interview for someone to decide whether you don't have the job. If you pass the 30-second first impression then you have the opportunity to prove your competence for the job.

Don't underestimate the power of a great first impression.

When standing up and speaking you want to look the part, you do not want the audience to be distracted by your loud patterned shirt or your five body piercings, unless that is the impression you have deliberately chosen.

Your professional image is also your reputation. I had a lady who expressed some interest in working with me on a couple of presentations. Her qualifications looked impressive, she seemed knowledgeable on the subject and had quite a lot to offer.

However, after being stood up at the first meeting we had planned as she did not mark it in her diary, I was sceptical. Then when we did finally have a meeting, she turned up in an old tracksuit when it was scheduled as a business meeting. When she kept using excuses for why she had not done what we had set, enough was enough for me. The first meeting disappointment alone had already started an impression about her organisational skills. I could not work with someone with that professional image. Not only was it annoying and disrespectful but working with someone who does not display a good professional image will create an association with that person in the eyes of others.

Your professional image is built over time – protect it at all costs and be aware of the things that you could do to damage it.

So if you are in a position to stand up and speak and want to create a professional image ensure you are the person you are proud of.

Not everyone wants to or needs to wear a suit when they are speaking, you may just choose to wear bright colours all the time. Some people will have to wear a uniform or it has been requested you wear something that ties in with the theme of the day. Whatever you choose to wear when you are presenting always make sure it also aligns to your style, your reputation and the image you wish others to remember you for.

Commitment To Your Message

Earlier in the chapter, we discussed being passionate about your topic. But being passionate sometimes is just not enough – you need to be committed to your industry or topic.

How do you display this commitment?

Many speakers have been involved in their topic or industry for many years. They have shown a commitment over time to developing their skills and knowledge in the area they are speaking on. In the professional arena of speakers, some may have written books, got a degree or have been working tirelessly for a cause over many years.

If you have been asked to speak to a group of customers about a product, how do you show commitment to that product? Do you use it yourself? Do you take it home for your family to use?

If you are asked to speak to your staff about the direction of the company and how they all need to think long term and you have recently resigned and will be leaving in two weeks, how do you think your presentation will go?

Your audience wants you to be passionate and committed to your product, information, cause and message.

Your credibility statement and your introduction usually reveal some insight about your commitment but you can also build and weave stories into your presentation that demonstrate your commitment.

Remember, you need to be authentic. A speaker who has a message about a new shampoo on the market – a shampoo that he states is the breakthrough in shampoo formulas – would have to be using that shampoo in order to be seen as authentic and committed to the product.

When you also show your audience that you are continuing to learn about your topic, it also shows your commitment.

Be committed or don't stand up and pretend you are.

Dare To Be Different

So you are getting to know yourself, why you are speaking, who you want to be, how you want others to perceive you, how to create and maintain your professional image – but now we get to the stage where I am challenging you to be different.

Now don't get confused between "different" and "not professional" or about not being yourself – it is about your competitive edge. This is about finding out what is unique about you. This is about looking at your strengths, or something you have that could be developed into a competitive-edge strength, and using it, marketing it.

Do you just want to be another presenter who stands up, says their thing and goes home and everyone comments that it was just another training programme or just another salesperson?

Or do you want your presentations to be memorable? Do you want your presentations to be talked about? And better still, do you want to be invited back to do and say more?

Think about famous people or unusual products – what makes them different? What makes them stand out?

Bill Gates, Princess Diana, Billy Connelly, Oprah Winfrey, Anthony Robbins, Jim Carey, Steve Irwin.

These are a few people who stand out for me. I didn't have to research anyone, I just thought of some people who stand out as being different. They are different for many reasons and that isn't the point. The point is they didn't try to be anyone else, they knew who they were and they put themselves out there for all to see.

They focused on their uniqueness and it is their uniqueness I remember them for, their qualities that make them stand out from others.

When you speak do you want to be a stand-out person? It doesn't mean you want to be famous, far from it – it means that when you speak you are not the same as every other speaker and people will remember who you are.

So, when you stand up to speak, find out what you can do to be noticed.

Some examples for you to think about:

- A speaker who wears a different hat every time they speak
- A speaker who uses a certain kind of music at every presentation

- A speaker who has a very strong accent and talks about it

- A speaker who has had a really unique life and uses stories about that during their presentation

- A speaker with one leg. I don't suggest you cut off a leg just to be different...

- A speaker with flaming red, long curly hair

- A speaker who sings through their presentations

- A speaker who really is the global expert

- A speaker who uses the audience in a unique way in their presentations

- A speaker who is known simply as "Smiley" because they have the biggest smile

- A speaker who wears the same outfit every time they speak

You see, being different doesn't mean you need to spend the next 10 years developing a marketing identity. It could be something as simple as your hair or your unusual taste in music.

Find out what makes you unique and work with it.

Share your message, be you, do it with your own style. But do try to be memorable.

I know I said this was going to be easy and we are only halfway through the book. Some of these things will develop over time. The more times you speak, the better you will become. The more times you speak, the more comfortable you will feel presenting in your own special way, and the more confident you will become taking a risk with your uniqueness and presenting something in a way no one else has.

Do not try to use every tip from the book the very first time you speak and then beat yourself up because you were not a speaking superstar. Being a great speaker is a journey, it is a skill that develops over time.

You can't expect to read a book on surfing, read all the rules, the tips and how to develop your own surfing style, then jump into the waves with your surfboard and be a world class surfer or even be able to stand up on the board the first time.

It is about practice and making mistakes and enjoying the journey along the way.

Speaking is the same. Read, practise, present, read, watch others, present, present, listen to feedback, present etc... To really develop a skill it takes many years of practice.

My husband always says that I am an expert speaker as I have not stopped speaking since we met. I am sure that we have all had lots of practice speaking and communicating so we can take a few years off our apprenticeship.

Find out what makes you unique and work with it.

Using Humour

This section is going to be brief and straight to the point.

If you are not an expert joke teller, don't tell jokes in a presentation.

Many people who present are under the impression that they have to be funny and being funny means telling jokes. But being funny isn't about the jokes you tell, it is about you being you, saying off-the-cuff lines when and if you have the appropriate opportunity to do so.

It is no secret that people like to enjoy themselves and people in a conference, a classroom or the boardroom are no exception. People who laugh are happy, people who are happy don't want to get up and leave, they are enjoying themselves. If people want to stay in your presence, it is because they are enjoying the experience. They are also there to listen to your message.

There are many ways to engage your audience.

- Interesting information
- Audience interactions
- Exciting props
- Visuals
- Music
- Unique stories

And humour is just another tool we can use to engage the audience and make the presentation an enjoyable experience.

When using humour don't try to force it out – the one-liners that present themselves just at the right moment are usually the most powerful.

You may be a naturally funny person who uses lots of humour throughout your presentation. It could be a strength you have and you use it well as part of your unique style of presenting.

Do not worry if you are not a naturally funny person. Sometimes allowing others to be funny in your audience still gives your presentation a touch of humour.

A lot of presenters cringe when they get a class clown but others use the class clown to their advantage to add a little humour.

The more relaxed you are the more relaxed you are about using humour. Give yourself permission to use humour. Think about when you are with your family and friends enjoying yourself. Are you having a laugh? Are you contributing to the funny stories and laughter? This natural humour that you use with family and friends is usually the same humour that your audience will find funny too (I guess depending on who your friends are...)

With that in mind, never use humour that may offend or upset anyone in the audience. There is sometimes a fine line between funny and offensive so be very careful with your choice of words and topics when deciding to allow humour into your presentation.

Sometimes your audience can be forgiving if an unintentional one-liner comes out, sometimes not.

I had a class recently – a group of adults completing a training qualification. I had this group for 10 days and this was on their first day – they were just getting to know me and I was just getting to know them and I slipped up with a very inappropriate one-liner.

As they were in my classroom for eight hours a day, I would encourage them to leave the classroom to have a break, especially over the lunchtime period, and take a walk or sit in the park, anything to have a break from the classroom.

As I was explaining this to my new class of professionals I finished by saying "so go out and enjoy the sunshine and spread your legs". I meant to say "stretch your legs".

What's worse was that I had no idea what I had just said until the shocked faces in the classroom were looking at me before bursting into laughter. Thank goodness they were forgiving. However, every lunchtime for the remaining nine days they all told me they were going out into the sunshine to... well you know what they said.

I think very carefully now when I describe what I want my students to do during their lunchbreak.

Your Stories

What I just told you about my lunchtime advice to my students was a story.

It happened to me, no other speaker or trainer (that I know of) will tell my story. I can tell that story and 1000 others just like it because they are mine. A participant in the same class may tell it, but it will be different as it will be from their perspective – perhaps even funnier.

One of the very best ways to connect with an audience is by the use of your stories – stories chosen to suit the occasion, stories chosen to suit your audience.

Speakers can use examples, they can give you facts and figures and handouts of research, but what moves people is people. People are real. Stories are accounts of people and their experiences.

Every speaker or presenter has led a different life to every other presenter. Your stories are what make you unique. You can tell them from the heart, you can tell them with an excitement that no other person can because you have lived it or seen it or experienced it.

I could stand up and tell a group of people about the research done on mothers' intuition. I could show you a PowerPoint presentation showing a chart and some statistics about some famous hospitals saving the lives of children because of mothers' intuition. It may in fact be a wonderful presentation that moves the audience and persuades them to donate to the research.

But when I tell my story about my son who was just two weeks old, sleeping in his pram for six hours and not waking up for his usual feed, he just kept sleeping...

When I tell my audience that I phoned hospitals and doctors and just kept getting told the same thing that some babies just sleep more than others...

When I explain to my audience about how I was feeling and how I felt an overwhelming fear that something was wrong with my baby and nobody would listen...

Then the audience is feeling my pain and frustration, I am connecting with every mother – maybe any father, grandparent or anyone who has cared for a baby.

And when I go on to tell them that I listened to my intuition and drove an hour with my baby and stood in the doctor's waiting room telling them I wasn't going anywhere until a doctor looks at my baby... The audience is really on my side.

But when I tell them that I finally got to see the doctor when my baby son was in complete heart failure... The audience is shocked and moved.

This is my story of mothers' intuition. No charts and statistics will move the audience in the same way. (By the way, my then two-week old baby son then went on to survive four open heart surgeries and has just celebrated his 18th birthday and is just like any other gorgeous teenager. Woohoo!)

I could then link my story to statistics and medical research.

This story about the strength of a mother's intuition is a real story, authentic, from the heart, but with a clear message – a message that no PowerPoint Presentation is ever going to compete with.

Now stories do not have to be heart wrenching or intense, they can be light and funny.

You can share a story as a customer going into a small family store and being ignored for over 10 minutes before walking out and going to their competitor over the road and being greeted by a friendly 16-year-old and then being introduced to the owner of the store personally where you proceeded to purchase a plasma screen, a dishwasher and a new fridge. You can then tell the story of how you told your mother-in-law about how friendly they were and that she should get a quote for her new washing machine.

A simple story about customer service.

Stories give your presentation a "realness". You are not just entertaining, educating, informing or persuading, now you are sharing snippets of people's real lives and how the topic you are discussing has had an impact on them.

When choosing a story you have to make it relevant.

Would I tell my story about my son to a group of executives looking at team building strategies? Of course not, it has no relevance. I would however tell a story about how my team achieved its goals even though we had 50% of the team down with the dreaded lurgy. Or I would tell them the story of how I hired a team with no skills just a great attitude and how the team outdid our competitors with all the right skills.

Next time you start to plan your presentation and start at the computer with your PowerPoint software, stop and have a think about what other ways, what powerful ways, you can use to get your message across.

I have put this section about stories in this chapter because it is all part of You Are the Expert in Being You.

The best thing is, you get to choose what stories about your life you wish to share.

You are not just *an* expert, you are the only expert in the world in being you.

So use who you are and all you have experienced to present with passion.

Be so good they can't ignore you

Steve Martin

7. TAKE THE FLOOR

So you have been asked to speak. You have spent the last three weeks preparing – your opening, your gestures, exactly how you will stand when you tell your story. Your PowerPoint presentation has been perfected.

Because you are so well prepared the nerves are at bay and you are ready to take the floor.

You arrive early to ensure you have everything you need in place – and then it happens.

You see it, a stage. It is huge and high. It is miles away from the audience. The lights are so bright. You are watching the current speaker. Oh no, she is standing behind a lectern. The microphone is on the lectern and it gets worse – the laptop is backstage. The speaker only has a remote to click to the next slide.

The panic now sets in. The way I have planned my presentation is described below:

- Walk to middle of room for my big opening line
- Talk about my few years in the research department
- Present my first slide – a slide that has to revisited later (but that's alright because I know how I can do that on any laptop by pressing the number of the slide and enter)
- During my presentation I have some items to hand out to let the audience members touch and feel them
- I have my flip chart with me to demonstrate some other items
- I have planned my movement
- My big ending must be done exactly where I started in the middle of the room

The stress is now overwhelming. I will not be able to do anything I had prepared. The whole presentation has to be done from behind a lectern with no laptop and it is too late to do anything about it as I am on in 10 minutes.

This is such a typical scenario for a person who is not a professional speaker or for someone who is not presenting on a regular basis.

There is so much preparation that goes into the presentation.

One of the major things all presenters must do so they can take the floor is find out as much as possible about:

- The venue
- The programme
- The audience
- The backstage professionals

The Venue

- The parking
- The type of venue (big hotel, boutique hotel, auditorium, offices)
- The catering
- The style of venue – formal or casual

The venue is an important factor. The type of presentation and function will depend on the type of venue chosen for the event.

If it is a small sales presentation it may be in a boardroom in a central office location. If it is a workplace training session it may not even be inside. The venue could be on a mining plant or in a kitchen. If it is a guest speaking motivational speech it could be at a prestigious hotel as they want the participants to feel spoilt.

Find out the reason why the particular venue has been chosen. It may give you more of an insight into the audience and the outcome expected.

The Room

- Is it inside or outside?
- Type of room
- Seating arrangements
- Room set-up (around tables, theatre style, standing)
- Lighting and temperature

Like many other factors, the room set-up can make or break a presentation.

If you are planning some interaction, a theatre style set-up where all the chairs are in rows will be difficult. The only interaction you may be able to include for the audience is having a chat about things to the person sitting next to them or directly in front or behind.

If you want to have group discussions or group activities try very hard to get your audience in groups with round or square tables set up.

If you need your audience to write but do not need any interaction with each other a horseshoe or a U shape is a great choice of set-up.

If you are the speaker and all eyes will be on you for the whole time then choose a theatre style.

Many corporate presentations are delivered in a boardroom – several people around the boardroom table and you standing at the head of the table. Usually all the members of the audience are seated, with access to pen, paper and other resources you may have prepared and presented to them.

If you are the person setting up the room for your presentation think about what you want your audience to do during your presentation and set the room accordingly.

Ensure factors such as the temperature of the room are not distracting issues. Don't put heaters on too high so everyone gets sleepy.

If your audience has a view out of windows that look out onto a busy mall, close the curtains or the blinds.

If you are not the one setting up the venue see if your requests can be accommodated if there is time. For example, your presentation may be after lunch so a few tables can be changed around during the lunch break.

The room set-up is a vital element in any successful presentation.

Your Space

- Stage or floor
- Podium, lectern or not
- Microphones
- Lighting on you
- Access to your resources

Let us explore your space. Your space within the room.

In the ideal perfect world you are not stuck behind a lectern (a stand where the microphone is and a place for your notes and sometimes big enough for your laptop too). You have a lapel microphone and you are free to move anywhere in the room or anywhere on stage. You have access to your resources whenever you like during the presentation and if you are presenting a big screen presentation you have a great remote.

Many good presenters do not have their entire slide show presentation in order. The slide show has been designed so you can go back to the first slide when a point is made or a question is asked. Or it has been designed so it can be adjusted according to the type of audience you have. Or you have a button to press that plays music if someone has a fantastic answer or comment.

Sometimes you may have to insist, without being pretentious, that you have access to your resources – although the technicians are wonderful people, you do not want to be in a position where you are blaming the technician for missing your favourite music on cue.

Also consider the lighting. If you have not presented on a large stage before, the bright lights and not being able to see your audience can be a bit of a shock. If there is a rehearsal or a time to hop up there beforehand, grab the opportunity. The more comfortable you are in your space the better.

The more you can own your area the better. Sometimes you may have to accept that this is what you have to work with. Other times, if it is crucial to the success of your presentation, you may absolutely have to insist on items. Remember your professional reputation too and know when not to sweat the small stuff. You want to be professional but not painful.

The Programme

- What is the schedule for the whole day?
- Who else is speaking and on what topic?
- When are the breaks?

You may be the person who is presenting for the whole day and your presentation is the whole event. But many other times you may be speaking for just a session of a whole day or at a three-day event.

You need to get as much information about everything else and everyone else that is happening at the event.

Who else is speaking and on what topic? Could you imagine following a sensational speaker who just spoke on team building and the main points of your talk are just what the last speaker's talk was all about.

What if your presentation is about resilience in the workplace and you decide to add some stress management into your talk but have not told anyone as a surprise but the next speaker's talk is on stress management? You also want other presenters on your side not just the audience. At this type of function it is a whole team approach and the organisers and the speakers need to work together collaboratively for a seamless and professional event.

You may be able to work in with other presenters and use their talks effectively, linking your talk in with the last three topics delivered.

It helps to know when the breaks have been scheduled, if there is a special guest, if there is a competition running or any other information that you may need to keep the audience on your side.

The bare minimum is requesting the timetable and programme of the event as early as you possibly can.

Audience Dynamics

- Who are they?
- Their expectations
- Prior knowledge
- Age, gender and nationality mix may also have to be a consideration

Your audience. There is a saying that there is no such thing as a bad audience, only bad presentations. This is a much argued point with anyone who speaks, teaches or trains people for a living.

I do believe you can have interesting characters in an audience and some audiences will respond differently to the same presentation than others, but I have yet to have a really bad audience.

A key success factor in any presentation is to know your audience before you get there. An audience that is presented with suggestions on how they should embrace the vision of the organisation during a talk on team building just after the company has announced a restructure and fired the manager may have good reason not to want to participate. The presenter may come away saying it was a difficult audience. Not a difficult audience at all, just a presenter who didn't know the audience.

If you are a presenter, what strategies or systems do you have in place to find out as much as you can about your audience before you are standing up in front of them?

If you are a trainer or instructor you may have carefully constructed enrolment forms, or a presenter may ask management about the other presentations the group has attended for the year.

If you can't get any information you may choose to ask some general questions to the audience and they can answer by a show of hands before you get stuck into the journey of your presentation. Or arrive early and meet as many of the audience as you can and maybe you can get an idea of the current issues of the day.

Once you know who is in your room then you need to try to cater for everyone in your audience.

We talked about learning styles in chapter 4 and how we should cater for all learning preferences. In Honey and Mumford's model they are:

- The Activist
- The Pragmatist
- The Reflector
- The Theorist

But we now have something else to factor in: Personality.

There may be someone in the room who just doesn't like you. There could be a class clown, or a person who is always interrupting or challenging everything you say. Or what about the person in the audience who is always talking to the person next to them and doesn't seem to be listening? What about the loudest person in the room who is also the most negative? What about the over-enthusiastic learner who asks for more information about everything you say?

How do you manage the dynamics of an audience?

The more experience you get the more comfortable you will be in your own skin and the more confidence you will have in your presentation and interacting with your audience.

Remember to come back to the positive self-talk too before you think the audience is against you before you even start. Is this audience really a group of hungry lions ready to pounce on you at the first opportunity or is your audience a wonderful group of people, who have come together to listen, learn and enjoy your presentation, a gift from you to them?

Once the right frame of mind has been achieved, then think about how each person in the room is an individual and that every person will come away from your presentation with something a little different.

See if you can use their strengths and try not to see their character as a presentation liability.

Use the class clown to put a bit of humour in your day. Ask them a question and expect a humorous answer and build it into your presentation.

Thank the person who challenges you by saying how wonderful it is to have someone in the room who is thinking outside the box and then go on to answer or discuss the comment.

The person who is constantly talking? They obviously like to talk so talk to them and get them talking to everyone not just the person beside them.

Presenters usually hate a "know it all" in the audience but what happens if they actually do know it all? What knowledge can they share in a group discussion?

And the one who always wants to be the leader? Well give them something to lead and praise their leadership skills.

Although you are the presenter, try to remember that every person in the room knows more about something than you do. Everyone in the room has a story. Everyone in the room will have something valuable to share. Everyone in the room is different to you.

You may not get a chance to let everyone have their say and share their stories, however, you should always make time to let your audience know you are there for them and the best way to get them on your side is to value their contribution.

Generally speaking the audience is on your side unless you move them to the other side. They want you to succeed. They want you to be left with a good impression of them – just as you want them to be left with a good impression of you.

The Backstage Professionals

- The name of everyone
- The equipment being used and set for the day
- The important people to remember and thank
- The technician… the person you want to know

In fact, not only the technician but anyone who is involved with the backstage essentials. The person who puts out your resources, the person who provides the refreshments, the person at the sales counter can have a lot of pull with customers after your event if you are selling any of your products.

Remember, events can't happen without all the people who work backstage. Get to know them all, they are the people worth getting to know. If you are working in a small office or training company or you are the wedding MC, who are your backstage people? It could come right down to the wait staff who are serving the food on the day. Get them on your side and they may just hold off clearing the dishes for five minutes, until after your big powerful closing.

And always remember when sending thankyou notes or expressing gratitude to include all the people who have helped your presentation be a success.

Just Ask

Wow – lots to think about before you start to prepare your presentation isn't there?

Why? Because you do not want to experience the first scenario of getting there and, within 10 minutes, having to prepare an entirely different presentation.

Some simple strategies put in place when you are asked to present can save you looking unprepared and unprofessional.

The thing we do is, we ask. Simple isn't it? We just ask.

Have a list of questions ready to ask so you do not have to call and annoy the organiser 20 times (you don't want to be too high maintenance). Many event coordinators will provide you with most or all the information that you need. Some speakers and trainers will have a letter or a checklist of their preferences or requests already prepared to give to the client or the technicians. Other presenters will send/email through a list of questions. Others will just phone and speak to the coordinators personally to discuss the set-up.

You can also do your own research of the venue. On many occasions, when it's been geographically possible, I have had a quick look at the venue beforehand just so I can get a feel for the place before I start planning or when I still have enough time to make adjustments.

Most coordinators will welcome your questions and will accommodate your requests as it is just as important for them that the event is a roaring success.

The message here is ask – ask about all these essential elements so you can walk in feeling confident about your presentation and knowing there are no devastating surprises.

Perfect Planning Includes Plan B And C

This is not to say if you do all your homework it will all be perfect every time.

I once went overseas to present to a number of companies. During my trip I was asked to attend a networking function for women. The right questions were asked, the answers came. I even had a typed schedule from the person who had organised my trip.

I thought I was attending a networking session with a group of ladies to discuss small business and local and international opportunities. A casual get-together over afternoon tea with likeminded women in a different country.

I arrived and I was introduced to a few very nice ladies and we were just starting to get into some deeper conversations and it was announced that we would be moving into the other room very soon for "Paula's presentation". My heart missed a beat or two, actually it was closer to 10. "Presentation? What presentation?" I was thinking. "There has not been any mention of a presentation from the planning stage two months ago until this very second."

I thought to myself, "Do not panic. I have a USB in my handbag with a few presentations on it, I'm sure I could work something out. Don't panic, but now is a good time to start fishing for answers without sounding like I don't know what I'm doing". I am now thinking I missed something in my notes. What if this is my fault? I started with the lady next to me.

"So, what are you wanting to get from today's presentation?" I asked with a big smile and pleading eyes.

"I'm not sure," she said. "What are you presenting?" This was not getting easier.

So I asked if I could have a quick look at the room set-up before we went in.

It was two rows of chairs and a long podium/catwalk and on top was a long table with chairs. It was set up like a panel. No screen in sight, no laptop, no microphones or flip charts.

It was at this time that I spoke to the coordinator about what she thought the ladies' expectations were of today. And much to my relief it was just to have a chat to me about how I had survived in business for many years and how I juggle my work/life balance. The word "presentation" was used loosely – it was still a little different to my schedule and my expectation of the function but it worked out really well in the end.

As a presenter you have to be able to think on your feet. As organised as you and everyone else may be prior to any event, unfortunately, unscheduled mishaps, miscommunication or complete disasters do occur.

A microphone may stop working, only 20 people show up and everyone was expecting 100, or the venue could be changed at the last minute due to a number of reasons beyond your control.

Be as prepared as you possibly can but expect the unexpected, and have plan B and C in your briefcase for the "just in case".

The Spotlight Is On You

Now let's get back to you taking the floor and owning the floor. Here are my favourite four tips to help you once you get there.

Tip #1 Move With Purpose

Don't walk from side to side and pace because you want to keep moving. Walk from one side of the room to say a piece from a story then move to the other side to tell everyone about a different character or different time in the story.

If you are using three Key Messages, you can move to three different areas of the room or stage to discuss each one.

If you are going to move, move with purpose. It is very distracting to watch someone swaying, dancing, or moving around the room so fast that people can't concentrate on what you are saying.

When you are performing a dance routine, you choreograph your every move, you plan where you will start, where you will be 10 seconds into your performance and exactly how you will do it and where you will be for the big finish. A routine should also be rehearsed. Delivering a presentation is the same. You may not be as methodical as a choreographed dance routine but you still need to plan your moves, rehearse your moves and always move with purpose.

Tip #2 Centre Yourself For Strong Points

Centring yourself means not only being in the centre of the stage or the room but also finding a strong stance yourself – a commanding position where you are standing still and confident. You may want to do your opening in this position, your key points and your powerful closing.

Tip #3 Don't Get Stuck

Try anything and everything not to get stuck in one position that restricts you from audience interaction or purposeful movement.

If you are stuck behind a lectern – and sometimes you may be – use your slides, your voice and your hands (still with purpose) as effectively as you can. Being stuck on one spot for an hour means you have to work extra hard to be engaging with your voice, your words and your stories.

Tip #4 Posture, Eye Contact, Smiling

When I was teaching modelling, public speaking and performing, the three performing points, as I used to call them, were Posture, Eye Contact and Smiling. In fact it was the first topic we covered for our students on day one, first lesson. With these three communication strategies, anyone, regardless of age, can look confident and approachable.

> **Posture**: Standing tall and walking tall with your head up and shoulders back gives you grace, an appearance of high self-esteem; it says you are a confident individual – a must for every speaker.

> **Eye Contact**: When you are performing or communicating in any aspect you should always look at your audience. Not at the back of the room as some suggest but at their faces – you are talking to them, you are connecting with them, you are trying to build a relationship with the audience. You can't do that by looking through them or over the top of their heads, so maintain eye contact throughout every presentation. When speaking to a large audience you can still lock eye contact with so many people in a short amount of time. Make people feel you are talking just to them, performing just for them.

Smiling: Smiling is a universal language. If you are smiling you are presenting a happy, relaxed and welcoming person. A smile is inviting. A smile makes you approachable. A genuine smile is warm, trusting and friendly. Even if the topic you are speaking about is a very serious topic there will always be room for a smile before, during and after your presentation.

Put these three performing points together, Posture, Eye Contact and Smiling, whenever you walk into a room, when you are meeting a new client, when you need to be displaying exceptional communication skills, and of course whenever you take the platform. Try it walking down the street, you will be amazed at how good it feels too.

Your Voice

Your voice can be an asset or a liability.

The way you use your voice can be the difference between a dynamic and a not-so-dynamic presentation. You may do everything else I am suggesting you do in this book but if you do not use your voice effectively you may not engage your audience. And engaging your audience is everything.

For those who know me I am quite a loud person. In fact, anyone who knows me when they are reading this line will laugh out loud and say that is an understatement. I have to be very careful that if I walk into a small classroom of 12 people I don't project my voice so it scares the life out of them. My voice is an asset in an energetic presentation with lots of people in a large room without a microphone. The difference is, I know my voice, so if I am using a microphone I need to speak much more softly, or if I am in a smaller room with a few people I need to tone it down a notch or three. But occasionally I can still throw out an overzealous presentation and have to take the cue from the audience (usually the looks on their faces) to move into a quieter zone.

Think not only about the volume of your voice, but your pitch, your use of inflections (change of tone), how fast you talk (another one of my controlled habits or not so controlled in a social setting). How much expression is in your voice? What facial expressions and gestures do you use when vocalising?

As a presenter or anyone who speaks, your voice is a tool of the trade, like a chef using his knife or a masseuse using his hands. A tool of the trade is something you need in order to do your job effectively.

You also need to care for your tool. Your voice is the most important tool you will need to do your job effectively. Look after it, value it, maintain it and train it.

The first thing you should do is listen to yourself. I have suggested in chapter 6, You Are the Expert in Being You, that you video yourself. For only your voice, close your eyes and listen if you are viewing a visual recording of yourself, or just tape your voice so you can hear what others hear.

You still need to be you, so don't go out and try to learn that beautiful London accent your best friend has or try to change the way you sound altogether. You are you and when you speak you want it to sound natural.

If you notice you have some bad habits, find yourself a voice coach if you really want to improve. However, it could be your unusual accent or your voice that makes you uniquely you.

The most important thing to recognise is that your voice is a valuable asset and your vital tool of the trade if you wish to be an engaging presenter.

Using A Microphone

Whether you will be expected to know how to use a microphone will depend on your role and when you need to speak. When I was teaching public speaking I was constantly amazed that when someone was asked to say exactly what they had just said but this time on the microphone they felt that the rules had changed – that somehow, what I was asking them to do now was not the same. All of a sudden the confident speaker looked nervous, uncomfortable and as if I had asked her to do something which would cause great pain. Once my classes got used to using a microphone it was just another item in the classroom.

People think that the microphone has this power to change the way they speak. The purpose of a microphone is to ensure everyone will hear your important message.

Try not to avoid using a microphone. It would be a waste of time for everyone, speaker and audience, if you chose not to use a microphone because of nerves and then most people didn't have a chance of hearing the whole presentation.

Try to practise with a microphone as much as you can so you feel comfortable with them.

Hand-held microphones are easy to use but they can restrict the way you naturally want to move because you are holding on to a microphone. Imagine having to have a microphone in one hand, the remote control in the other and trying to present naturally.

When you have a choice or an opportunity to make a request, ask for a lapel microphone or a headset.

Here are a few tips when speaking into a microphone.

- Speak in your natural voice – you do not need to speak louder, that is what the microphone is there to do

- Do not have a hand-held microphone, or a microphone in a stand, in front of your face when you are speaking. Position it just underneath you mouth

- Be careful not to speak and blow air into the microphone. Some words, especially the ones starting with P, tend to have more air expelled when producing the sound and the air projects into the microphone

- Prior to arriving, find out which type of microphone you will be using and ensure you are dressed appropriately. For example, if using a lapel microphone where will you attach it? I was told embarrassing stories from another professional speaker who regularly witnessed instruments having to be attached to ladies underwear as there was nowhere else for things to be attached

Your microphone is an aid, not part of your presentation.

Plain Talk

I recently read an article in our state newspaper about the language some of our politicians and high flyers use when speaking to the media or delivering presentations.

There were so many examples of high intellect, extensive use of the English vocabulary, industry jargon and an impressive arrangement of words. After reading the 10 or so examples I really didn't know what they were on about. In fact, that is what the whole article was about. Presenters get so caught up using big words and industry jargon that the layperson has trouble understanding what the Key Messages really are.

You could say "Pop into the store and buy the product, as you can see it's fantastic" or you could say "It would be appreciated and a highly recommended strategy if you could find the address of my store in the area of Midland. Upon your decision to enter the store, being fully informed about the product in question, as we have shared the benefits and uniqueness of this innovative ensemble with you today, you could take it upon yourself to remove the product off the display area and move forward towards the zone 3 register area to make a purchase".

Get my point? Keep it simple.

Yes, you must use language aimed at the correct level for your audience but don't get caught up with the urge to use every word in the dictionary unless you are giving an English tutorial to a conference full of PhD students.

Use simple messages, taglines to remember, and always use language that everyone in the room will be able to understand.

The only limit to your impact is your imagination and your commitment

Tony Robbins

8. OTHER STUFF TO SUPPORT YOUR DYNAMIC PRESENTATION

The magic word here is *support*. You are the presentation.

There are so many mediums now for people to get information so why do they want to sit in a room and listen to you? Why wouldn't they want to receive an email or watch a webinar or visit the company blog? Or how about the company intranet?

They can just surf the internet, research and access information from all around the world. Why do people enrol in face-to-face courses instead of completing one online from the comfort of their own homes?

Many people, including me and the other millions around the world, like the real thing. We like the human connection, the feeling of being present, the opportunity for face-to-face communication with the presenter and the other people attending. Nothing will ever take its place.

So, if the audience has come to your presentation to see you, why would you put all your information on a big screen in the middle of the stage or room while you stand second to the giant document you are presenting?

Visual aids are there to *support* your presentation never to be your presentation.

You are the centre of the presentation. You are there to educate, entertain, persuade or to toast the bride and groom personally. Could you imagine being asked to say a few words about the birthday boy and you give a handout or a list for everyone to read or you project a few words on the big screen in bullet point? It would just not be acceptable. Different perhaps, but not acceptable. However, you could start the speech with one of your stories about the birthday boy and then show a photograph on the big screen to visualise a major point in your story. The big screen would be used so everyone could see the photograph at the same time and it would support your speech. It is in no way your speech. You blank out the photograph and you continue with your story and your celebratory toast. All eyes are still on you, the presenter.

Let's look at how we can use a few visual aids and other creative ways to engage your audience, to get your message across.

Script Or Notes

How are you going to remember everything in your presentation?

This one question alone is enough to make any new speaker suffer from speaking anxiety. What if I forget everything? Should I read from a script? Should I use palm cards?

When we were at school our English teachers would highly recommend we use palm cards to remember our speech. Palm cards are small cards that fit in the palm of our hands with Key Messages or sentences on them. After each section of the speech we would put that card at the bottom of the pack until all of the topics written on the cards had been presented.

The point of this of course is to ensure no one ever read from a script or tried to remember a script word for word – both a recipe for disaster, and a fine way to dampen your credibility as a subject matter expert.

Anyone can read from a script, so why are they paying you? Your head and eyes are developing a relationship with the piece of paper instead of your audience.

So many speakers try to remember a speech word for word and sometimes they pull it off but most times when one word is forgotten the speaker goes into panic mode as they are now out of sequence. Scripts are for the theatre. You learn the words from your script and then, if you forget your lines, your prompt is waiting in the wings to whisper them to you and help you get back into your sequence. A presenter is not there to read lines, a presenter is there to present a message. So, no scripts allowed.

Some presenters will use palm cards, most presenters will use notes or other reminders to keep them on track and ensure that all of their presentation is presented in order and no important topics are missed.

If you are using a laptop, some programmes will have a screen with your notes to one side so you know what slide is coming up next and you can type notes beforehand to assist you with the topic discussion when the slide is presented. The audience cannot see your notes, only the slide you are presenting.

If you are standing behind a lectern you have a place to put your notes and you can look down occasionally to see if you are on the right track.

You may have pre-written flip charts, props in a certain order on the stage to keep you in sequence, or you could be one of those presenters who ensures the Key Messages are in the right order but they talk in response to audience needs and reactions.

If you have written notes or palm cards, always number the pages or cards. If you happen to drop your notes as you are walking up to deliver your presentation (oh, yes – this does happen!) then it's easy to sort them into order again. It's not a good idea to spend five minutes trying to put your notes back into sequence because you haven't numbered them – or worse, delivering your presentation in the wrong order...!

I always find that I have notes in writing big enough for me to see (the size is getting bigger every year). My notes are usually key words in the order of my presentation. I can write those notes on my laptop or, when no technology is involved, I have them on my resource table, my lectern or somewhere I can access them if I really need them. Most of the time I do not need them but they are there if I am having a moment of "Who am I? Why am I here? And who are all these people?"

That's not to say you shouldn't rehearse. Rehearsals are a must – in the shower of course. I usually rehearse my opening, my Key Messages and some of my stories. My whole presentation never comes out exactly the same in every rehearsal though; in the real world it is never exactly the same. Your audience may determine which stories you use, or something funny may have happened to you at morning tea and you want to share it.

Rehearsing could be a form of security for presenters for the "just in case".

Do not use your slides as the only way to keep you on track. I have seen this done by so many presenters and it is obvious they have no idea which slide is coming up next. Read on about what your slide show is really there for and what it isn't – it isn't there to be your notes or your script.

Whatever method of reminder you choose ensure it does not interfere with the way you present your information. The notes and reminders are there for you, not for the audience to see if you are on track.

You may experiment for the first few times and see what works best for you.

Visual And Audio Aids

Visual aids are for people to look at to help them internalise the information. Some people learn better visually just like others learn better by listening. An audio aid could be sound effects, music and audio tape. It is essential we stimulate as many senses as we can for deeper learning.

We are now going to explore visual and audio aids which enhance our presentation.

The Big Screen And Powerpoint

When I was first training, we used overhead projectors and transparencies – I thought that was pretty sensational. We used flip charts, butchers' paper on desks, pre-prepared posters and anything we could think of to engage our learners creatively.

Amazingly enough some of the old methodologies are proving much more effective than some of our new modern technologies.

Then there was PowerPoint. It was amazing. When PowerPoint first came into play, most of us would prepare presentations in a manner which reflected how good we were at using every animation in the programme. There were words flying in from all directions, there were 100 bullet points per page, there was the sound of engines and aeroplanes. What PowerPoint didn't do wasn't worth doing.

The thing was, although all of my participants also thought my presentations were fantastic, at the end of the day when I asked what they had learnt, they had learnt about how great my PowerPoint skills were. Great for my ego, not so great for the purpose of my presentation.

How many presentations have you been to with the slide show as the star of the show?

Before you go rushing into using PowerPoint, or any programme that displays slides on a big screen, decide why you are using it.

The overuse or the ineffective use of PowerPoint has become so bad over the years that some conference organisers have declared their events PowerPoint-free zones. This way the chosen presenters actually have to present.

You may have also heard the terms "death by PowerPoint" and "I've been PowerPointed to sleep". The thing is PowerPoint is an exceptional programme when used correctly. The best book that I have read on presentation design – and I have read a few over the years – is Presentation Zen by Garr Reynolds. A brilliant read from the first page to the last. I highly recommend you purchase the book and use it as a guide for developing truly amazing slides.

Tips for slide shows

- A slide show is there to support your presentation
- Use photos and diagrams to demonstrate your point
- You can jump from slide to slide whenever you want by choosing the slide number on your keypad and enter
- Don't walk in front of the screen and don't leave it on when you don't need it – press the B button on your keypad to blank the screen
- Use a remote. This way you are free to walk the stage or room and most functions will be available on a good quality remote
- Don't use 101 animations unless they are necessary
- Think about what you want to display – a document, a graph or a picture – to support your story
- Do not put too much information on your slides
- Use contrasting colours so your audience can read the text
- Don't let the slides lead your presentation – always know what slide is next and why you are using it
- If your slide show technology fails, you should still be able to deliver a powerful presentation

Flip Charts

I tend to use flip charts and butchers' paper more and more now in my workshops and classrooms. Flip charts are great for interactive sessions, to demonstrate a point, for participants to use. They are also great to stick to the walls after use as a reminder of what the class is working on.

Whiteboards can be used in the same manner but unless you have an electronic one it is difficult to record the work you have just done on it.

Remember a few tips for these mediums:

- Use quality paper – So no seepages on to the next page
- Use quality pens – Thick and bold markers
- Use colour – Think of your paper as a poster you are designing
- Use size – Size does matter, everyone in the room should be able to read the information
- Use a title or a heading on every chart
- In a classroom, stick the charts around the room
- Avoid using flip charts in big audiences as they may not be able to see it

Films And Recordings

Short films and clips are fantastic to use in your presentations. Always ensure they are relevant to the topic and ensure you are aware of copyright terms for usage in your presentations.

You can make your own short clips to show, you don't always have to buy them. If you are presenting an induction programme for a company, how great would it be to show the company video and some interviews with their staff? Or, if you are presenting a customer service workshop, it would be good to present a short film on terrible or great customer service in a real workplace environment.

Audio recordings are also great. Instead of a handout, you could give a CD to a participant to listen to before or after the class to reflect on the presentation, or you could choose to play a recording in class.

When choosing your film clip or audio recording ensure:

- It is relevant
- It is of good quality sound and picture
- You are aware of copyright restrictions of use

Handouts

Handouts can be anything from additional information, marketing material, take-home worksheets, participant manuals, or gifts.

Unless the audience needs their handouts during the presentation, try to hand them out towards the end of the presentation. You want them to be listening to you not reading and looking at the gifts you have just presented to them.

Some presenters do not give handouts of their PowerPoint slides. The belief is that they would make no sense without the presenter. I tend to agree. I sometimes prepare some "Key Points from Presentation" handouts for them to take home. It is entirely up to the individual presenter and I would only ever give them out after the presentation or I sometimes email them out if they leave their details/business cards with me.

If you do hand out material to your audience, ensure that:

- It is professionally presented
- It has your contact details on it
- It incites curiosity so they will be directed to your website or company for more information
- It is current

- There is something in the handout that encourages them to keep it or pass it on – free tips, a discount voucher, a calendar of events etc

Props

Props are items that are used to enhance your presentation.

If you were doing a magic show you would have many props to get your message across. If you were demonstrating a new product you would have the product and other items to assist in your demonstration.

Sometimes, props can be on stage to set a scene. For example, if you were a world champion surfer talking to a group about setting goals, you may have a surfboard on stage with you. You may be talking to your audience about good nutrition and on a table there may be many examples of food that support your Key Messages.

Props are also visual aids so think about what you can use or bring on stage to enhance or support your message.

You can also use props to get your audience interacting. A set of juggling balls for each table, a product to pass around, a food sample to taste. Using props for audience interaction can stimulate many senses and can bring them to a deeper level of understanding, not to mention that using props can also be a way of introducing fun and laughter into your room and a great strategy for audience engagement.

Props are valuable because:

- You have something to show
- You have something to see, touch, smell and in some instances taste
- You have a strategy to get the audience involved

- You can set the scene
- You can provide proof

Music

Music, like a smile, can be a universal language.

Many presenters could not imagine presenting without music.

Music can fill a room with joy or sadness, excitement or anxiety.

Music in a room can prompt us to dance, to sing, to remember.

Music is a powerful medium.

You can have a lot of fun with music in your presentations, regardless of your particular taste in music. Like any other aid you bring into your classroom, think and decide what it is for. Is it just to lighten the mood, is it a cue to come back after a break, or is it just because you like classical music before you go on stage?

You can use music for memory, to shock the audience, to relax them. It could be a great "get attention" strategy, which is then linked into your presentation.

Music can also be used to:

- Create a mood – Remember though, music can be personal and what makes you feel light and happy may make someone else feel annoyed
- Get people up and moving
- Share a song
- Demonstrate a point
- Have reflection time during an activity
- Get your audience's attention

Games

Games can be powerful. Games can be a disaster waiting to happen. Games can get your audience on your side. Games can alienate your audience.

A lot of presenters will bring games into their presentation or workshops.

Games must be relevant. Using a game for team building, like how to build the biggest tower out of a pack of cards in the shortest amount of time, could work really well.

You could play a version of "Simon Says" to suggest that it is not what we hear but it is what we see that has impact.

There are many books about games and ice-breakers that you can use in your presentations. It is just another method that can be used to get a message across or another way of inviting laughter and fun into presentations. You just need to ensure you think about your message and whether a game is the right way, or the best way, of getting your message across.

If you are going to use games, keep in mind:

- They must be relevant
- Know your audience
- Introduce them at an appropriate time in the session
- Ensure that the game will not offend anyone
- Do not insist that everyone must join in

Another speaker

You may decide to use another speaker to support your presentation.

This may be an invited guest; someone who can share their real life story with the audience to get the message across; a client who loves using your product; a person who has used all your strategies to become successful.

Inviting a guest speaker to talk about you or your Key Messages gives your message a different dimension. The audience can have another point of view, another supporter of the message.

You may decide to work with another speaker/presenter because you believe you have different strengths or different expertise that would be the perfect combination for this style of presentation.

When working with another presenter always choose someone you know you can work with. Always choose someone who understands and is committed to the Key Messages and the purpose of the presentation. Choose someone who will rehearse with you and will have the same views on professional image.

If you are up there with a presenter who does not share the same views as you about all these things it could be a direct reflection on you as a presenter too.

If you can work with a likeminded soul, it can be fun and the synergy between presenters can be a highlight of the presentation. You can direct humour at each other, you can have a helping hand interacting with the audience. You can discuss each other's strengths openly with the audience.

"We are so lucky to have Fiona on our team. She is the most energetic and hardworking person I have ever worked with." Brilliant coming from the presenter beside you.

If choosing to work with another presenter, ensure:

- They have the same commitment
- They know about professional image
- You rehearse
- You have the same agenda
- You can work together successfully
- You enjoy the experience

Over the years, presentation aids will come and go, and presentation trends and new technology will be introduced. The one presentation tool that will never be a trend or go out of style or be adjusted with new technology will be you.

You – the most powerful and entertaining presentation tool available.

Ensure that you are always centre stage to any other supporting tool you decide to introduce.

Don't wait until everything is just right. It will never be perfect. There will always be challenges, obstacles and less than perfect conditions. So what. Get started now. With each step you take, you will grow stronger and stronger, more and more skilled, more and more self-confident and more and more successful

Mark Victor Hansen

9. WHAT IF IT ALL GOES TERRIBLY WRONG?

As much as we read and learn about how to do it, when to do it, where to do it, why to do it, sometimes, just sometimes, things happen that are totally out of our control. It could be a power cut, a difficult client, too many people in the audience or, heaven forbid, no one turns up at all.

Other misfortunes could be: Going totally blank just as you are introduced; your heel breaking; or what if you have brought the wrong slide show with you? (I took the wrong trophies to a student graduation once – I was so organised then just picked up the wrong box when I was flying out the door. Disaster...)

Just like any other job or activity, things can simply go wrong.

We don't want to focus on the negative incidents but you do need to develop good contingency management skills. Presenters need to "think on their feet". Good presenters will not get ruffled and go to pieces when every small detail, or perhaps even a big detail, doesn't quite happen the way you planned. It is about bouncing back, moving on and doing the best you can with what you have at the present time.

Read on for some of the events that could go terribly wrong and how you can deal with them.

The Time Of Day You Present

Remember the last time you went off to a training course or a seminar. How did you feel straight after lunch? Or how about at four o'clock in the afternoon? I know by 4pm I am feeling a bit drained, especially if I have been listening and learning all day. What about at 9am in the morning? Are you feeling motivated and open to new ideas? Are you alert and ready for anything?

As a presenter, the time of day you present information is crucial. Many times you just will not get a choice. You have been invited to speak at 4.30pm, prior to the end of the day, and you have accepted. You just need to be aware of how your audience may be feeling at that time of day. How can you make your message more interactive, interesting and exciting so they don't fall asleep?

Sometimes, after lunch your audience may feel a little bloated and lacking energy. This is a great time to use ice-breakers if you are in a classroom, or perhaps introduce an energetic music quiz for a larger audience. If you are in a sales meeting why not bring out the product to touch and feel, and present some startling statistics?

Imagine being asked to be a guest speaker at a dinner. Your slot is 9pm for 30 minutes and you have just realised that the 40 members of the audience have been there with a wine or two or three since 4pm. Recipe for disaster.

When agreeing to speak or present, find out as much as you can, including the time of day you will be presenting. Find out who is speaking before you and after you. Find out if you will be presenting during lunch or dinner. The sound of clinking cutlery could also be a distraction.

Whatever the answers are, you just need to be prepared. The more surprises you have before you enter a room to present, the more your nerves can take over. The time of the day can impact on your presentation so be aware and plan some strategies to overcome any issues.

The Speaker Before You

If at all possible, arrive to watch as many presenters prior to your presentation.

A couple of things could happen here. What if the last speaker was terrible? What if the audience is falling asleep? What if the presenter didn't have all the facts and basically just did a very average performance?

It could be great for you as you walk on to the platform, prepared and structured with all the ingredients for a powerful presentation.

However, you may have to do an audience diagnosis and perhaps major surgery to the audience to prepare their minds and bodies for your presentation. You may have to pull out of your toolkit an unplanned ice-breaker to get your audience back even though it wasn't you who lost them in the first place.

Always remember though if the last presenter was awful, and they may know it, they could be feeling quite upset to say the least. Ensure you never, ever make a comment about the previous presenter, or any presenter for that matter, in a negative manner. Always support other presenters and find a positive comment to say about their presentation.

So let's look at the other hand now – what if the last presenter was inspiring, incredible and got the audience to a standing ovation?

It is your first time presenting and you have to follow a guru. Yes, that could be enough to set the nerves rolling again. All the things that would be going through your head: "The audience will compare me; how can I be expected to compete with that? Will the audience even want me on stage now?" Awful self-talk again... but we are only human and this self-talk may creep into your mind.

My tip here for following an awesome speaker is *use it*. Use the energy in the room. The people in the audience are now inspired, they are open to new ideas, they are now waiting to be inspired again... no pressure of course.

The strongest position you are in is: "You are the expert in being you". Be yourself.

Compliment the last speaker. This will get the audience on your side. Move forward to your own presentation. If the previous speaker had some really interesting points, you can refer to them to emphasise some of your own points. Always reference another speaker or researcher/author though. Never claim the work as your own.

If all the presenters on the day are great, the audience will be happy and satisfied, and you would have been involved and been a major contributor to a highly successful event. No negatives here.

Technical Difficulties

This is one of the most common issues that I think every active presenter has experienced at some time. It can be as minor as your slide show presents a word or two in a slightly different format on the big screen or as major as everything you prepared doesn't work at all.

The more prepared you are and the more questions you ask about the technical side of things, the fewer surprises you will have.

If possible, arrive early and do a sound check, a compatibility check and ensure any equipment and resources that you wish to use have been pre-tested and are doing everything you want them to do. If something is not going to work, at least it gives you time for Plan B and C. It is very unprofessional to be playing around with technical or backstage equipment in front of a waiting audience.

If something goes wrong with the technical side, move on. If there are people around to help you, you need to delegate the task and get back to your job – presenting.

The audience does not want to watch you watching someone else fixing a blown bulb in a data projector. Be with the audience, instigate a group discussion, take an unscheduled break, move to another part of the presentation that does not require the projector. Just never, never ignore your audience or spend the next 30 minutes apologising for the terrible circumstances.

You Just Suck

That's right. Your presentation just sucks. That is the technical term for: Your presentation was not something to be written about in a positive manner in the Presenter of the Year magazine. Your ego is now shattered.

Even the most seasoned presenters have bad days. Just as an artist has an exceptional painting, they also have average paintings; or a plumber forgets some of his tools and drove 100km to a job he just couldn't fix, leaving an irate customer.

Sometimes you just can't get the words out or the audience is a bit flat and all of your great ice-breakers or one-liners that have worked before aren't having any impact. Other times you think an activity will be well suited to the objective and it just doesn't work.

It will be your resiliency that comes into play here. Your ability to bounce back. Not the "I was so embarrassed, they will never ask me to speak again, I will have to leave the country so I don't have to face anyone in that room again". I am sure that sometimes you think it is worse than it actually is. It is more about your damaged ego.

I remember presenting to a group this year and what was meant to be a short, inspiring talk turned into a debate about the topic, lead by a heated member of the audience. My perfectly rehearsed closing was now just inappropriate, my Key Messages seemed to be lost and I was glad when it was all over.

In my eyes it was a disaster. I didn't think I would ever be invited back to this crowd. The first comment I got from an audience member was that it was great there was so much audience interaction and how I let them all have their say about the topic.

Unbelievable.

Did my presentation go to plan? No. Did I suck? In my eyes, yes... but not completely in the eyes of the audience.

But if it's a case of you the presenter and the audience being on the same page with the "the presenter sucks" thinking, learn by it and move on. Try to analyse what went wrong and how you could do it differently next time. Don't try to blame anyone, just accept that you didn't have a great day at work and you will be having a better day tomorrow.

Go home, find someone to pamper your ego, get a good night's sleep and just accept that you are human too.

Feedback

Essential, essential, essential.

It doesn't matter if you are going to be presenting for the first time or this is presentation 573. We are always learning and improving. Feedback and evaluation is essential if you ever want to improve, be in tune with your audience and give them what they really want.

You can get feedback in a number of ways. The most common is a feedback form or I fondly call them Happy Sheets as I am being optimistic and hoping all the comments on the form will make me happy. You have probably filled out a Happy Sheet or two over the years. They are the forms that usually have a rating scale on them (quantitative data) and ask you things like: On a scale of 1-5 (1 being the highest) did you enjoy the presentation? Did it meet your expectations?

Many Happy Sheets also ask you for suggestions and what your thoughts are (qualitative data) like: What was the most important topic for you today? Which strategies from today's presentation will you share with your work colleagues?

When constructing a Happy Sheet think carefully about what information you are looking for. If you are a new presenter or trainer you may want to include more about your delivery and your style. If you have been presenting for years, the feedback form may be geared to get constructive feedback about the information or the venue and not as much about the presenter.

If you do not ask for feedback you cannot know what your audience is thinking.

Some presenters find it quite confrontational so they just don't do it. They will never improve. You need to look at the data and the comments and take on board what you need to.

If you have 100 people in the audience and 99 are totally happy with the content, do you change it for one? Of course not, but take note of their comment. It could be they are from a different department than everyone else so the information was not relevant. So next time you may decide to run a separate session for different departments if the same comment keeps coming up from only person not from that department.

The information you receive is invaluable and if you are a trainer, just a part of training best practice.

Feedback doesn't have to always be that formal. You may think it inappropriate to ask your audience to fill out a feedback form at a sales meeting or a wedding so anecdotal feedback is just as good. You may not even get the feedback from the audience, it could be from their boss or even their clients.

Feedback sometimes isn't instant either, you may get a comment six months later from an audience member who implemented your new system, saying how much more profitable their business has been over the past period because of it.

Evaluation and feedback is continuous, just like your own personal and professional development. If you want to always be in demand, ensure you never stop learning and improving. So seek feedback from your clients, your audience, your peers, your friends, your family – anyone who has an interest in your development. You can also collect testimonials from really happy clients to use in your marketing material.

If you are seeking coaching or assistance with your presentations always choose someone you respect as a professional. Choose someone whose style you like. Choose someone who shares the same values as you and someone who only has your best interests in mind.

So What Else Can Go Wrong During A Presentation?

You name it, it could go wrong. You could even get a flat tyre on the way to the presentation before you even start. It's not about what can go wrong, it's about being aware that things could go wrong and developing the skills to be able to overcome obstacles.

Oh, and for the trophy disaster at the graduation… I didn't know about it until I was on stage in front of 800 people starting to read out the first name and realised I had tomorrow night's trophies. I had to admit my mistake while standing on stage and promised to personally deliver the trophies to the students the next day. Lucky I could remember the names along with the help from another instructor so they all got to come and stand at the front of the stage for a big applause. Was it the perfect end to a great night? No, I made a big error. Did it change my life? Not at all, and most people in the audience that night just accepted a busy working mum – with all the best intentions – running out the door and making a huge mistake. Did I kick myself for it, was I embarrassed, did I feel terrible? Absolutely.

For more reading on being able to rise to the challenges set before us, pick up the book What to Say When…You're Dying on the Platform by Lilly Walters, a very funny but great resource for all those moments.

10. FROM OTHERS WHO HAVE DONE IT AND SURVIVED

This section includes stories from real presenters who actually go out and do it, from the Pro and the Active to the Truly Terrified. They have conquered nerves, obstacles and other incredible circumstances to be able to stand up, speak out and share their messages.

You won't hear from just the Professional speaker – because most of you won't be professional speakers – but it is great to get an insight from someone who actually speaks for a living. Someone who has developed their presentation skills to such a level they are in constant demand to educate, inform and persuade clients all over the world. You will also read about the Active speaker with an amazing personal story – a story that will inspire you to overcome any nerves that serve no purpose. Not everyone is a relaxed presenter as you are probably aware so take a tip or two from the Truly Terrified who is just embarking on a new career as a trainer and has struggled with public speaking terrors all his life.

All three stories will have something to share that will touch a nerve, move your emotions, get you moving and, hopefully, give you the inspiration to stand up and tell your message.

Over the years I have met hundreds if not thousands of presenters, trainers, teachers, speakers, sales and marketing people, CEOs, just people who tell their message. People from all walks of life.

The common thread with so many of these people is they have a message to help others. They want to share their messages, tell their stories, show their products so others can benefit. They want to teach, to share, to educate, to inspire. There are always a few out there who speak to feed their own egos but the majority of people who have a desire to speak have a common goal. The goal is to make a difference.

Learn the art and skill of how to present. And make the decision to be one of those people who can make a difference.

My three presenters over the page have.

The Pro:
David Koutsoukis

I have been a full-time professional speaker for eight years, but I guess I have been "on stage" for roughly 30 years. In previous lives I have been a teacher, an outdoor adventure instructor, a musician, team leader and a television personality (I was one of Fat Cat's offsiders on Children's Channel Seven and Earlybirds in the late 80s/early 90s). I would have been in front of an audience of some description or another more than 3000 times.

I became a full-time speaker in 2002 and supplemented my income by singing in pubs two nights a week. I earned $17800 from speaking in my first year and it has gone up exponentially every year since then. I distinctly remember a speaker named David Penglase telling me "the best way to make it in the speaking business is to stay in the speaking business!"

As a general rule I speak about 100 days per year – a speaking day being any day in which I speak – from a one hour keynote to a full-day programme. This is a number that I have found I am comfortable with.

The mix of speaking I do is roughly 30% keynotes, 30% leadership and team building retreats , 30% in-house training programmes and about 10% public seminars.

Out of the 100 days I present, typically I would do 50 of those in my home town of Perth, about 20 in regional Western Australia, 20 in the eastern states and about 10 internationally.

This mix works really well for me as I like variety and I enjoy travel. I try to incorporate family holidays into three of these engagements each year – one intra-state, one inter-state and one international.

I must admit that I do not get nervous before a presentation. Any anxiety I have is mainly about the equipment – will the PowerPoint show work properly? Will the sound be okay? Will the speaker before me finish on time? I guess there are a number of reasons I don't get nervous. Firstly, I've been speaking long enough to know what works and what doesn't; secondly I've been on stage in a number of capacities thousands of times; and thirdly, I am a very organised person and make sure everything is ready to go. I arrive early to set up and make sure everything is okay, and I am prepared for things that might go wrong. I once remember reading that "self-belief is in the preparation" and I have a positive self-belief up on stage because I am always well prepared.

I love speaking. I believe I was born to teach. Whether it's to be the centre of attention, or the satisfaction I get when my audience gets that "aha" look in their eyes, or whether it's the feeling I get when I see people laughing and enjoying themselves at one of my events, I'm not sure. It's probably a combination of all of the above. I just know that when I'm in front of an audience it "feels right".

An element of my personal vision is "to be able to do what I want to do, when I want to do it, and with people I want to do it with" and I would say that I'm about 80% there. So, I guess you could say I look forward to 80% of my speaking jobs. I don't dislike the other 20%, I just don't get excited about them. I love travelling and I love new experiences, so I particularly look forward to speaking in new places or to new audiences. My two favourite speaking engagements are: Conferences, where I usually pick up some inspiration for myself; and leadership/team building retreats, where I can really get to know people.

One of my favourite mantras about speaking is: "It's not what you say, it's not what you do, it's how you make them feel that counts". So, the first thing I want to leave my audience with is a great memory of an enjoyable experience. Secondly, whenever I'm in an audience I not only want to be inspired – I want some useful, take-home tools or strategies. Consequently I like to give my audience "plug and play" information – something they can take away and use straightaway. For example, a useful tool I use is the Click! Colours Personal Discovery Tool, and a useful strategy I might share is "to build relationships in your workplace use each person's name at least once every day".

To any aspiring speakers, I offer three pieces of advice.

1. When you are on stage – does it feel right? If it does you're on the right path.

2. Find your passion and purpose and speak about it. If you do you'll never have to "work" another day in your life. Unless you know your passion already it can take a few years of trial and error to find out what you "really" want to speak about.

3. Remember that "the more you do, the more you do". There is no fast track – you need to spend a few years "treading the boards" before you become a polished professional. There is no substitute for speaking in front of an audience.

So, go forth and speak – as much as you can!

The Active Speaker:
Peter Dhu

As a teenager and young adult I stuttered badly and struggled to speak. I was ridiculed, teased and mocked at school. I survived these high school and university years by being an elective mute, writing down on paper every request, every communication, so that I would not face the humiliation, embarrassment and shame of stuttering. Yes, it was that bad.

My first job saw me placed in the basement with no client contact and strict instructions not to answer the telephone under any circumstances. Over five years, I trained many new graduates, only to see them leapfrog over me and continually be promoted to senior positions. When I confronted my boss, I was told bluntly to be grateful for the job I had and, because my communication skills were so bad, to not ever expect to be promoted so "Please Stop Applying for Senior Jobs".

Since that time I have devoted time and effort, sweat and tears, to overcome my stutter and learn to speak fluently. I have pushed many boundaries and faced my disability and fear.

Now I public speak at every opportunity.

Over these years I have helped and trained thousands of other people to overcome speaking and communication difficulties. I have served as president of the Australian Speak Easy Association for five years and as president of the Speak Easy Association WA for seven years.

Because of my journey and my newfound speaking ability, I am now lucky enough to have the opportunity to travel and speak in conferences and conventions around the world including Australia, Denmark, Belgium, Canada, England, Ireland and Croatia.

My mission and passion in life is to help people find their voice so that they can effectively and confidently get their message and their point of view across to others. To achieve this I have moved into public speaking training and coaching and I also speak to inspire others. I talk about achieving success, learning from experience and taking ownership of your own destiny.

I continue to speak at every opportunity and I currently speak two to three times a week. Not bad for a teenager who wouldn't speak at all. Before a presentation I now have no nerves or anxiety at all. I just get up and be myself, not worrying if I stutter or not, because I know that I am more than just a person who stutters. I continue to get great satisfaction and enjoyment each and every time I speak. When you receive positive feedback from the audience, it is really very rewarding.

I feel a bit of a charlatan, getting paid to speak. It is a bit like paying a diabetic to take their insulin or an asthmatic for taking their inhalers. I must speak to stay fluent, to stay healthy, to keep my stutter at bay, the same as the diabetic and the asthmatic. But I have the cheek to get paid for it.

I show the audience that anyone can achieve what they want and personal success should not fall by the wayside because of self-doubt, fear, and negative stereotypes. If I can stand up and speak before an audience, then anything is possible.

The Truly Terrified:
Kevin Tibble

No, No, No – I thought this course was about training and assessing, not public speaking. I can train and speak to one person at a time not a whole class. Now I have to get up in front of a class full of people I hardly know and speak. Not just for two minutes, no I have to speak for 15 minutes.

Two weeks of worrying: Sweats, shakes, nightmares, yes really nightmares. Nightmares about all the things that could go wrong. Every night a different curse. Why do I have to do this?

Bungy jumping, base jumping even, I could do those instead – anything but speak.

Waiting in anticipation, I receive my topic. My 15-minute presentation is something I know about – in fact, I could be the world expert. NERVES. I have to speak for 15 minutes on nerves. First step: Scan the internet. Must be some answers there, the world's knowledge at my fingertips. Maybe I can buy a programme to make the presentation for me. Can't believe there is so much on the fear of 'the speak'. It's obviously not just me.

D-Day comes, sit through ten presentations, can't remember any of them. I should have gone first. I don't recognise my own body, I can feel the sweat, my heart pounding, my head a blur. Need the toilet. No time. Here it is, I can't stop my foot shaking. Remember what Paula said – structure, include the audience, structure, take a breath, stick to the structure. Fourteen minutes have now passed. Almost there, some questions to answer. Not half bad, remembered the answers. Review time – (didn't die) positive feedback. Shock and disbelief, they enjoyed it. Someone could see my foot tapping through the whole presentation. Laugh to myself as both legs were shaking so much I thought I was going to fall over. Glad they only noticed my foot. My seat beckons. My legs start working as I walk back to my chair. Relief. Heart is slowing down. Calm.

What was I so worked up about? Breathing normal, bladder normal. Just as I am thinking I may not have to do that again, ever, we are told the next time is an hour.

Lying in bed that night reflecting on the day… Was it really that bad? Yes it was. Think I'll go bungy jumping next time instead...

Next time comes… little less nervous… foot stopped tapping, breathing a little easier, I know I will survive... adding a bit of humour now... who would have thought... after another 50 times I may even get to like it.

Success is not a destination that you ever reach. Success is the quality of your journey.

Jennifer James

11. TIME TO WOW YOUR AUDIENCE AND LEAVE THEM WANTING MORE

We've done it.

You are now at the end of the Speaking in the Shower pages and the beginning of your new journey – a journey to developing superstar presentation skills.

What did I tell you? No secrets, no mystery, just lots of tips and stories to help you over the line, to assist you in planning, structuring and delivering an awesome presentation.

Hopefully you will keep this guide with you and use it when you need to prepare and deliver your next presentation; to read some of the quotations and stories from time to time to give you inspiration; to share some of the strategies with your colleagues to help them be better presenters too.

It's time to put it all together. Time for action. Time to welcome the next opportunity to present your message.

Turn the water off and step out of your shower. You're holding your head high, the confidence is oozing from every pore, the opening line is on the tip of your tongue just waiting for an eager audience. Dry yourself off, dress to kill, spray on your favourite smelly stuff, charge out the door and step onto the platform.

You're on...

COMMON SPEAKING
TERMS: AFTER

Definitions of common speaking terms *after* you take the Speaking in the Shower journey – terms that you know and always use as a confident, charismatic speaker who seeks opportunities to speak.

Presentation – An opportunity to inform, entertain, educate, motivate and share a message

Audience – A wonderful group of people, who have come together to listen, learn and enjoy my presentation

Fear – Something not associated with my presentations

Sleep – What I do so well the night before a presentation to ensure my mind, body and heart are well prepared

Hyperventilation – Something the next speaker is doing after he has heard my awesome presentation

Lectern – A structure to stand behind when movement on your stage is restricted or not possible

Visual Aid – An additional prop to support my presentation

Presentation Opportunity – An opportunity to stand up, speak out and have my message heard. An opportunity to meet new people and build long-term relationships

Survival – A guaranteed natural occurrence after a presentation opportunity

Key Message – Your powerful message for your audience

Applause – The best sound in the world when I am standing in front of a huge audience

Name Recall – A skill that I need to practise to help me remember the names of my clients, audience members and anyone who is involved in helping to organise my presentations

PowerPoint – See Visual Aid

Credibility Statement – Who I am, why I am here and how I am going to help you

Humour – Essential ingredient of every presentation – natural humour of course unless you're an expert in telling great jokes

Presenter Style – Being yourself and being memorable

Presentation Structure – The essential strategy for a successful presentation every time

JOIN ME IN THE JOURNEY

If you have enjoyed reading Speaking in the Shower and would like to have some additional help to put it all into practice you can attend a Speaking in the Shower Workshop.

Paula Smith presents workshops for the new or not so confident presenter and more intensive higher order presentation skills for those who have done it all before and wish to take their presentation skills to a higher level.

Enrol in a public workshop or book a customised in-house workshop to ensure your key people will deliver an exceptional presentation every time.

Paula is also available for conferences and seminars.

Paula engages the audience and presents a number of dynamic and memorable keynotes and workshops.

For the executive or serious presenter, Paula offers a one-on-one coaching service and will personally work with you to develop your sensational presentation.

Contact Paula by visiting the Speaking in the Shower website.

www.speakingintheshower.com.au

Our deepest fear is not that we are inadequate. Our deepest fear is that we are powerful beyond measure. It is our light, not our darkness that most frightens us. We ask ourselves, Who am I to be brilliant, gorgeous, talented, fabulous? Actually, who are you not to be? You are a child of God. Your playing small does not serve the world. There is nothing enlightened about shrinking so that other people won't feel insecure around you. We are all meant to shine, as children do. We were born to make manifest the glory of God that is within us. It's not just in some of us; it's in everyone. And as we let our own light shine, we unconsciously give other people permission to do the same. As we are liberated from our own fear, our presence automatically liberates others.

Marianne Williamson

www.ingramcontent.com/pod-product-compliance
Lightning Source LLC
Chambersburg PA
CBHW071001040426
42443CB00007B/604